ELEMENTS: THE BASICS OF FAITH

DR. MICHAEL MAIDEN

JOSHUA GENERATION PUBLISHING

ELEMENTS: THE BASICS OF FAITH
Copyright © 2012
by Dr. Michael Maiden

ISBN-13: 978-0-615-65241-2

Published by
Joshua Generation Publishing
6225 N. Central Ave.
Phoenix, AZ 85012

CONTENTS

INTRO.

ELEMENTS: THE SIMPLEST PRINCIPLES OF A SUBJECT OF STUDY

This book is a simple introduction into the basic elements of biblical Christianity. Webster's dictionary defines the word ELEMENT as "the simplest principles of a subject of study." The nine chapters of this book each cover a crucial component of what it means to be a follower of Jesus Christ. As you discover what Jesus has done for you, what is available to you in His gifts and grace, what He's prepared for you to receive both in this lifetime and in the time to come, you'll not only grow stronger in your faith by understanding what it means to be "born again," but you'll live with a heart that is continually thankful to God for what He's given you.

Whether you're a new believer or someone who's known the Lord for some time, the examination and study of these vital elements will benefit and bless you greatly. If you're reading this book and have not yet experienced Christ as your Savior, Baptizer or Healer, then know it's not an accident you're reading this. This is your time to receive God's gift of salvation, Holy Spirit baptism and divine healing through Jesus Christ.

At the end of every chapter there is a series of questions for you to fill out and answer related to the previous topic. Take the time to answer each question. By doing so, you're affirming your clear understanding and agreement with what the Bible teaches is yours through Jesus Christ.

This book is divided into two sections. In section one we focus on 'The Person and Grace of Our Lord Jesus Christ.' There are six chapters in this section. Each chapter addresses who Jesus is and what He's done for us. These six chapters are an initial examination into the five titles of Christ and the five works of grace He has freely given mankind. If you hold out your hand in front of you and look at it, I'll give you a simple example and memory tool related to these five points of grace. First, look at your thumb. It is the most essential part of your hand in that all the other fingers are completely dependent on it for almost every use of the hand. The thumb represents Jesus Christ our Savior who brings the gift of salvation to all who believe. Next, the index finger represents Jesus our Baptizer. After salvation we continue to follow the Lord in a two-fold experience called baptism. First, every person who receives Christ as their personal Savior is then commanded in Scripture to be baptized (immersed) in water, identifying with the death, burial and resurrection of Christ our Savior. Because there are two separate baptisms for every believer to experience, after water baptism, we are to ask and receive the baptism of the Holy Spirit. This Holy Spirit infilling is an irreplaceably essential experience that supernaturally empowers the life of the believer.

Our middle finger represents Jesus our Healer. Healing is a part of God's provision for us through the grace of Jesus Christ. The fourth finger (ring finger) represents Jesus our Provider, whose grace includes provision for our earthly needs. Our fifth finger (pinky) represents Jesus Christ our Coming King. The Scriptures reveal the promise of Jesus Christ coming back again to claim His bride (all believers).

The second section of this book is titled "Three Essential Elements for the Life of Every Believer." These three chapters will cover: 1. The Word of God, 2. Prayer, Praise and Worship, and 3. The Church. This section deals with the lifestyle of a believer and what it takes to be successful as a follower of Christ. While you're reading and studying these three chapters, begin to apply what you're learning to your life. The Word of God works in our life when we work it into our lifestyle and behavior. Don't just know the truth about God's Word, prayer and the local church, but live in the truth by spending time in the study of God's Word and in prayer. Don't just learn about the importance of what the church is, find and participate in the life of a Bible believing and teaching, Christ-honoring and Spirit empowered local church.

Following Christ is life's greatest adventure! It is a never-ending, never boring, life-giving and heavenly rewarding journey with God Himself as your guide and partner. This is what this life is all about: Knowing and following Jesus Christ. Everything else in the world pales in comparison to this great truth. This is the reason we're alive. This is the purpose and meaning of what life was designed to give us – a living, personal relationship with God that begins now, but will last for eternity. Let the journey begin!

1 JESUS CHRIST OUR SAVIOR

THE PERSON AND GRACE OF OUR LORD JESUS CHRIST.

JESUS CHRIST IS OUR SAVIOR. HE GIVES THE GRACE OF SALVATION.
The first element of what Christianity is all about is also the most important one. Everything else about being a follower of Christ hinges on the foundation of this irreplaceable cornerstone of truth: Jesus Christ came from heaven as God's Son, became a man (born of a virgin), lived a sinless life, suffered and died on a cross where all of mankind's sin was put on Him, was buried for three days, rose from the grave victorious, and ascended to heaven. He did all that for you and me! Let's now examine the reason and meaning in what Christ has done for us.

Why does mankind need to be saved? What does salvation mean to me?

When I talk to people about God and His love for them, many times they'll respond with the question "How could a just and loving God allow so much pain, evil, injustice and suffering in the world?" For many this represents a hurdle they've been unable to move past. The simple explanation to this thoughtful question is that the world as it presently exists is not in the same condition as when it was first created. It has been radically, negatively transformed by just one thing: man's sin. When God made the universe it was perfect in every way. When God created man, He made man to be immortal, perfect and God-like.

Genesis 1:31 (NKJV)
Then God saw everything that He had made, and indeed it was very good. So the evening and the morning were the sixth day.

Genesis 2:7 (NKJV)
And the LORD God formed man of the dust of the ground, and breathed into his nostrils the breath of life; and man became a living being.

We can only imagine what the world was like, what man was capable of before everything changed. There was no disease, no pain, no sadness, no death. All of creation, including the centerpiece of God's creation, man, was perfect in every way. God Himself rejoiced in the quality of His masterpiece ("And God saw that it was good." Genesis 1:10, 12, 18, 21, 25, 31). What was the event that so radically disturbed and disfigured this portrait of complete perfection? The answer is original sin. Adam's disobedience to God in the garden of Eden.

In Genesis 2:16-17 the Bible tells us:
And the LORD God commanded the man, saying, "Of every tree of the garden you may freely eat; but of the tree of the knowledge of good and evil you shall not eat, for in the day that you eat of it you shall surely die."
God had but one rule for Adam and Eve in the garden. They eventually broke that one rule.

Genesis 3:6 (NKJV)
So when the woman saw that the tree was good for food, that it was pleasant to the eyes, and a tree desirable to make one wise, she took of its fruit and ate. She also gave to her husband with her, and he ate.
What happens next is what we call 'the fall of man'. In other words, the severe and continuing consequences of Adam's sin have had a universal effect on all of creation, including mankind.

Genesis 3:16-19 (NKJV)

To the woman He said: "I will greatly multiply your sorrow and your conception; in pain you shall bring forth children; your desire shall be for your husband, and he shall rule over you."

Then to Adam He said, "Because you have heeded the voice of your wife, and have eaten from the tree of which I commanded you, saying, 'You shall not eat of it': "Cursed is the ground for your sake; in toil you shall eat of it all the days of your life. Both thorns and thistles it shall bring forth for you, and you shall eat the herb of the field. In the sweat of your face you shall eat bread till you return to the ground, for out of it you were taken; for dust you are, and to dust you shall return."

Mankind's access to a personal relationship with God and to eternal life were cut off by sins presence.

Genesis 3:22, 24 (NKJV)

Then the LORD God said, "Behold, the man has become like one of Us, to know good and evil. And now, lest he put out his hand and take also of the tree of life, and eat, and live forever"

So He drove out the man; and He placed cherubim at the east of the garden of Eden, and a flaming sword which turned every way, to guard the way to the tree of life.

The imperfect world we now see and live in is the direct result of the consequences of man's sin. Don't blame God for the mess we're in. He didn't create disease, pain, death, war, injustice or suffering. Our sin has. Our forefather, Adam's sin brought about the fall (when everything in creation, including man, lost its perfection and immortality) and since we're the descendants of a fallen man, we have inherited and continued the legacy of sin in our own lives and behavior.

Why do we all need salvation? Because we're all lost, fallen from God and incapable of escaping our dilemma without the rescue of a loving and forgiving God.

The Bible describes our common condition in these verses:

Romans 3:10-12 (NKJV)

As it is written: "There is none righteous, no, not one;

There is none who understands; there is none who seeks after God.

They have all turned aside; they have together become unprofitable; there is none who does good, no, not one."

Romans 3:10-12 (MSG)

Scripture leaves no doubt about it: There's nobody living right, not even one, nobody who knows the score, nobody alert for God. They've all taken the wrong turn; they've all wandered down blind alleys.

No one's living right; I can't find a single one.

Romans 3:23 (NKJV)

. . . for all have sinned and fall short of the glory of God,

Romans 3:23 (MSG)

Since we've compiled this long and sorry record as sinners (both us and them) and proved that we are utterly incapable of living the glorious lives God wills for us, God did it for us.

Romans 5:12 (NKJV)

Therefore, just as through one man sin entered the world, and death through sin, and thus death spread to all men, because all sinned

Romans 5:12 (MSG)

You know the story of how Adam landed us in the dilemma we're in— first sin, then death, and no one exempt from either sin or death.

Now some people struggle with being categorized and condemned as being 'sinners.' They think that, sure, maybe they're not perfect in every way, but overall they see themselves as good, not bad or evil people. When the line "that saved a wretch like me" in the song "Amazing Grace" is sung or heard, they can't identify with being a sinful wretch. Well, compared to all the really evil things done by really bad people, they see themselves as different, better, not really needing salvation as Christ offers it to all.

God knew we were easily predisposed to the concept of self-righteousness – pleasing God by thinking we're good enough to get into heaven. So His salvation was to give us the Law through the prophet Moses. The entire function of this heaven sent set of standards for mankind's behavior was to show us the unattainably high standards of God's glory and holiness, and then to convict all of us guilty as being incapable of fulfilling its demands.

Galatians 3:21-22 (MSG)

If such is the case, is the law, then, an anti-promise, a negation of God's will for us? Not at all. Its purpose was to make obvious to everyone that we are, in ourselves, out of right relationship with God, and therefore to show us the futility of devising some religious system for getting by our own efforts what we can only get by waiting in faith for God to complete his promise. For if any kind of rule-keeping had power to create life in us, we would certainly have gotten it by this time.

Galatians 3:11-12 (MSG)

The obvious impossibility of carrying out such a moral program should make it plain that no one can sustain a relationship with God that way. The person who lives in right relationship with God does it by embracing what God arranges for him. Doing things for God is the opposite of entering into what God does for you. Habakkuk had it right: "The person who believes God, is set right by God—and that's the real life." Rule-keeping does not naturally evolve into living by faith, but only perpetuates itself in more and more rule-keeping, a fact observed in Scripture: "The one who does these things [rule-keeping] continues to live by them."

Romans 3:27-28 (MSG)

So where does that leave our proud Jewish insider claims and counter-claims? Canceled? Yes, canceled. What we've learned is this: God does not respond to what we do; we respond to what God does. We've finally figured it out. Our lives get in step with God and all others by letting him set the pace, not by proudly or anxiously trying to run the parade.

The Bible tells us that if we're guilty in just one part of the law, we're guilty of failing every part of the law.

James 2:10 (NKJV)

For whoever shall keep the whole law, and yet stumble in one point, he is guilty of all.

James 2:10 (NLT)

For the person who keeps all of the laws except one is as guilty as a person who has broken all of God's laws.

God uses this law to convict and condemn all mankind, not because He's an angry old man in the sky, but we're united in universal condemnation so that we might then all qualify for heaven's unbelievable answer – being unconditionally forgiven by the free gift of God's grace through Jesus Christ!

Galatians 3:22 (NKJV)

But the Scripture has confined all under sin, that the promise by faith in Jesus Christ might be given to those who believe.

Galatians 3:22 (MSG)

Its purpose was to make obvious to everyone that we are, in ourselves, out of right relationship with God, and therefore to show us the futility of devising some religious system for getting by our own efforts what we can only get by waiting in faith for God to complete his promise. For if any kind of rule-keeping had power to create life in us, we would certainly have gotten it by this time.

The Bible tells us that Christ died for every person who has or will live in this world. He took our sins; He took our place on the cross of Calvary.

I Timothy 1:15 (NKJV)

This is a faithful saying and worthy of all acceptance, that Christ Jesus came into the world to save sinners, of whom I am chief.

I John 2:2 (MSG)

When he served as a sacrifice for our sins, he solved the sin problem for good—not only ours, but the whole world's.

John 3:14-17 (NKJV)

And as Moses lifted up the serpent in the wilderness, even so must the Son of Man be lifted up, that whoever believes in Him should not perish but have eternal life. For God so loved the world that He gave His only begotten Son, that whoever believes in Him should not perish but have everlasting life. For God did not send His Son into the world to condemn the world, but that the world through Him might be saved.

In His own words, Jesus described what He had come to accomplish. He said, "whoever believes" would be saved. That means everybody. That means anybody. That means you and me. He took our place, suffering and dying for our sin.

Isaiah 53:4-6 (MSG)

But the fact is it was our pains he carried—our disfigurements, all the things wrong with us. We thought he brought it on himself, that God was punishing him for his own failures.

But it was our sins that did that to him, that ripped and tore and crushed him— our sins! He took the punishment, and that made us whole. Through his bruises we get healed.

We're all like sheep who've wandered off and gotten lost. We've all done our own thing, gone our own way. And God has piled all our sins, everything we've done wrong, on him, on him.

Isaiah 53:10, 12 (MSG)

Still, it's what God had in mind all along, to crush him with pain. The plan was that he give himself as an offering for sin so that he'd see life come from it—life, life, and more life. And God's plan will deeply prosper through him.

Therefore I'll reward him extravagantly—the best of everything, the highest honors—because he looked death in the face and didn't flinch, because he embraced the company of the lowest. He took on his own shoulders the sin of the many, he took up the cause of all the black sheep.

II Corinthians 5:21 (NKJV)

For He made Him who knew no sin to be sin for us, that we might become the righteousness of God in Him.

II Corinthians 5:21 (MSG)

How? You ask. In Christ. God put the wrong on him who never did anything wrong, so we could be put right with God.

Salvation is God's free gift to you through Jesus Christ!

Titus 3:4-7 (MSG)

But when God, our kind and loving Savior God, stepped in, he saved us from all that. It was all his doing; we had nothing to do with it. He gave us a good bath, and we came out of it new people, washed inside and out by the Holy Spirit. Our Savior Jesus poured out new life so generously. God's gift has restored our relationship with him and given us back our lives.

Ephesians 2:8-9 (NKJV)

For by grace you have been saved through faith, and that not of yourselves; it is the gift of God, not of works, lest anyone should boast.

Romans 6:23 (NKJV)

For the wages of sin is death, but the gift of God is eternal life in Christ Jesus our Lord.

The Bible tells us that in salvation we are forgiven of all our sins by the redeeming blood of Jesus!

Ephesians 1:7 (NKJV)

In Him we have redemption through His blood, the forgiveness of sins, according to the riches of His grace

Psalm 103:2-3 (NKJV)

Bless the LORD, O my soul, and forget not all His benefits:

Who forgives all your iniquities, Who heals all your diseases,

Colossians 2:13-14 (NKJV)
And you, being dead in your trespasses and the uncircumcision of your flesh, He has made alive together with Him, having forgiven you all trespasses, having wiped out the handwriting of requirements that was against us, which was contrary to us. And He has taken it out of the way, having nailed it to the cross.

Colossians 2:13-14 (MSG)
When you were stuck in your old sin-dead life, you were incapable of responding to God. God brought you alive—right along with Christ! Think of it! All sins forgiven, the slate wiped clean, that old arrest warrant canceled and nailed to Christ's cross.

Micah 7:19 (NKJV)
He will again have compassion on us, and will subdue our iniquities. You will cast all our sins into the depths of the sea.

Micah 7:19 (MSG)
And compassion is on its way to us. You'll stamp out our wrongdoing. You'll sink our sins to the bottom of the ocean.

When you receive God's free gift of salvation your entire life is changed forever! God doesn't just forgive you, He transforms you into a whole new person with a new life. Jesus describes this metamorphosis as being 'born again.'

John 3:3 (NKJV)
Jesus answered and said to him, "Most assuredly, I say to you, unless one is born again, he cannot see the kingdom of God."

We're called 'new creations in Christ' in II Corinthians 5:17 (NKJV):
Therefore, if anyone is in Christ, he is a new creation; old things have passed away; behold, all things have become new.

The Greek word for 'saved' in the New Testament is sozo, which means "to save, heal, cure, preserve, keep safe and sound, rescue from danger or destruction, deliver. Sozo saves from spiritual death by forgiving sin and its effects and from physical death by healing. It means 'to give new life', 'to cause to have a new heart'." See how complete and all encompassing is God's grace that brings salvation to our lives!

How do we receive God's free gift of salvation? Salvation is for everyone. It is a free gift. The simple steps to receiving this incredible gift are given us in scripture.

> Romans 10:9-13 (NKJV, MSG) tells us:
> ...that if you confess with your mouth the Lord Jesus and believe in your heart that God has raised Him from the dead, you will be saved. For with the heart one believes unto righteousness, and with the mouth confession is made unto salvation. For the Scripture says, "Whoever believes on Him will not be put to shame." For there is no distinction between Jew and Greek, for the same Lord over all is rich to all who call upon Him. For "whoever calls on the name of the LORD shall be saved."

Say the welcoming word to God—"Jesus is my Master"—embracing, body and soul, God's work of doing in us what he did in raising Jesus from the dead. That's it. You're not "doing" anything; you're simply calling out to God, trusting him to do it for you. That's salvation. With your whole being you embrace God setting things right, and then you say it, right out loud: "God has set everything right between him and me!" Scripture reassures us, "No one who trusts God like this—heart and soul—will ever regret it." It's exactly the same no matter what a person's religious background may be: the same God for all of us, acting the same incredibly generous way to everyone who calls out for help. "Everyone who calls, 'Help, God!' gets help."

STEP ONE: Believe that Jesus Christ is Lord and that He died to forgive your sins and give you eternal life.

> Acts 4:12 (NKJV)
> Nor is there salvation in any other, for there is no other name under heaven given among men by which we must be saved."

STEP TWO: Confess with your mouth - Sincerely pray this out loud:

"Heavenly Father, today I admit that I'm a sinner in need of a Savior. Thank you loving God for sending Your Son to take away all my sin. I now receive this great gift of forgiveness. I turn away from my former life and surrender all I am to You. I thank you for the gift of eternal life in Jesus' name. Amen."

The Bible confidently declares that everyone who has ever made this sincere confession has immediately received everything God's Word promises to believers: Forgiveness of sin, the gift of righteousness, the Spirit of adoption, eternal life, abundant life, the Holy Spirit's indwelling presence, access to God's kingdom as revealed in the scriptures and much, much more!

As I close this chapter of the most important element in the life of the believer, I want to share a couple more thoughts on what God has done for you in Jesus. Some have wrongly concluded that man's sin, resulting in the fall, was an unforeseen difficulty that God had to suddenly respond to with a plan 'B' program. As if there were an emergency meeting of the Godhead (Father, Son, Holy Spirit) about what they should do now that their best laid plan had been disrupted by man's sin. But the Bible tells us that one of God's attributes is that He's omniscient (all-knowing) and that one of the attributes of omniscience is foreknowledge (knowing everything about the future). So why would an omniscient God, who possesses complete foreknowledge, go ahead with this plan to create the universe and make man in His own image knowing all the while that man would betray Him with sin? Knowing what it would cost Him, why? One simple word. Love. He loves us completely, passionately and unconditionally. He saw what would happen – foreknowledge.

Romans 8:29 (NKJV)
For whom He foreknew, He also predestined to be conformed to the image of His Son, that He might be the firstborn among many brethren.

Before the creation of the world, our Heavenly Father and His Son, Jesus, had a conversation something like this: "Son, do you see what will happen with man?" "Yes, Father, I see that man will sin against us." "Son, I'm willing to send you to rescue them, if you're willing to go." "I'm willing, Father."

Jesus is described in Revelation 13:2 as the Lamb slain from the foundations of the world. From eternity past God saw you, loved you, chose you, called you, and gave His Son to die for you. You are God's greatest treasure – His work of art.

Ephesians 2:10 (NKJV)
For we are His workmanship, created in Christ Jesus for good works, which God prepared beforehand that we should walk in them.

The Bible says this in Romans 8:29-30:
For whom He foreknew, He also predestined to be conformed to the image of His Son, that He might be the firstborn among many brethren.   Moreover whom He predestined, these He also called; whom He called, these He also justified; and whom He justified, these He also glorified.

You are predestined by God – handpicked and given destiny.

Ephesians 1:5-7 (NKJV)
...having predestined us to adoption as sons by Jesus Christ to Himself, according to the good pleasure of His will, to the praise of the glory of His grace, by which He made us accepted in the Beloved.
   In Him we have redemption through His blood, the forgiveness of sins, according to the riches of His grace

Ephesians 1:5-7 (MSG)
Long, long ago he decided to adopt us into his family through Jesus Christ. (What pleasure he took in planning this!) He wanted us to enter into the celebration of his lavish gift-giving by the hand of his beloved Son.
   Because of the sacrifice of the Messiah, his blood poured out on the altar of the Cross, we're a free people—free of penalties and punishments chalked up by all our misdeeds.

As a believer you cannot, nor do you have the need to, ever be 'saved' again. Salvation is a one time experience that never leaves or changes. But believers are people, and people struggle with sin. As a Christian, when you sin, God does not disown you, reject you or give up on you. The grace He has for us will always be more and greater than the sin we bring to Him. Grace never loses a battle to sin.

Romans 5:20-21 (NKJV)

Moreover the law entered that the offense might abound. But where sin abounded, grace abounded much more, so that as sin reigned in death, even so grace might reign through righteousness to eternal life through Jesus Christ our Lord.

Romans 5:20-21 (MSG)

All that passing laws against sin did was produce more lawbreakers. But sin didn't, and doesn't, have a chance in competition with the aggressive forgiveness we call grace. When it's sin versus grace, grace wins hands down. All sin can do is threaten us with death, and that's the end of it. Grace, because God is putting everything together again through the Messiah, invites us into life—a life that goes on and on and on, world without end.

How do we respond to God when we've sinned as Christians? God's grace has once again made a glorious provision for us to be granted continual relief from sin and its effect of separating us from God.

I John 1:8-10 (NKJV)

If we say that we have no sin, we deceive ourselves, and the truth is not in us. If we confess our sins, He is faithful and just to forgive us our sins and to cleanse us from all unrighteousness. If we say that we have not sinned, we make Him a liar, and His word is not in us.

I John 1:8-10 (MSG)

If we claim that we're free of sin, we're only fooling ourselves. A claim like that is errant nonsense. On the other hand, if we admit our sins—make a clean breast of them—he won't let us down; he'll be true to himself. He'll forgive our sins and purge us of all wrongdoing. If we claim that we've never sinned, we out-and-out contradict God—make a liar out of him. A claim like that only shows off our ignorance of God.

There it is. We're to confess sin, and then God will get rid of it! Don't let lingering seasons of unconfessed sin infect your life. The sooner we confess it, the sooner He removes it and cleanses us. When we're quick to admit we're wrong, He's quick to forgive us and make us strong!

God has always loved you. By experiencing salvation you have welcomed and received His great love. No one can take your salvation from you. No one can ever take you away from God's unconditional love. God now makes His home in your heart. He called you his own child. Salvation is not the end, but rather only the beginning of the glorious things He has for you. Like the great door into a vast and glorious palace, salvation is the door by which we enter into relationship with God and into the presence of His kingdom. Live with a passion to open all the new doors in this glorious castle of the kingdom. The Bible is your map and the Holy Spirit is your guide in this lifelong adventure of pursuing and discovering God and His glorious grace. Welcome to the greatest, most satisfying adventure of this life!

GLOSSARY OF BIBLICAL TERMS RELATING TO SALVATION

Salvation – The redeeming work of Jesus Christ to forgive man from all sin and restore us back to full relationship with God.
- Jesus Christ is God's Son (He's God). (John 3:16, Phil. 2:6)
- Jesus came as a man born of a virgin (sinless birth). (John 1:1, Matt. 1:18, 23)
- Jesus lived a completely sinless life (II Cor. 5;21)
- Jesus bore the sins of mankind on the cross. (Isa. 53:6, 10, 12)
- Jesus died and was buried for three days. (Luke 23:52-53)
- He arose from the dead on the third day (He successfully atoned for man's sins and conquered death). (Matt. 28:1-10)
- He ascended to heaven. (Acts 1:9-11)

Grace – God's Riches At Christ's Expense. Unmerited favor, free gift (Eph. 2:8)

Born Again – Phrase used by Jesus to describe what needs to happen to all men – a new heavenly birth when our dead spirits are regenerated. (John 3:3, Titus 3:7)

Redemption – When something lost is purchased or repurchased by a price. Our redemption was purchased by the greatest price ever paid for by anyone for anything – the precious blood of Jesus Christ. (I Peter 1:18-19)

Righteousness – The imparted gift of right standing with God through the blood of Jesus. (II Cor. 5:21)

Justification – Just as if I'd never sinned. The process by which our sins are removed through forgiveness and the gift of righteousness imparted to us. (Rom. 3:24)

The Fall – A description of the consequence of Adam's sin. All of creation, especially mankind has been radically, negatively reshaped because of one thing – the presence of sin. The world as we know it is not the same world God originally created. Sin has made a mess of what once was perfect in every way.

Omniscience – One of the attributes of God – to be all-knowing. (Isa. 40:28, Ps. 139:1-6)

Foreknowledge – An attribute of God's omniscience – Perfect knowledge of all things in the future. (Rom. 8:29)

Predestination – An outcropping of God's foreknowledge to know the future and thus to make plans, designs and destiny for those who will live in it. (Eph. 1:5) All believers are predestined.

Repentance – Literally – "to change the mind." We repent when we change our mind about sin, confess it to God and turn away from it. (Acts 3:38)

Jesus Christ – The second person of the triune Godhead. God's Son who freely laid down His divine attributes to become a man and then die for all mankind. He is both the Creator of the world and the Savior of the world. His victory complete, He is now seated at the right hand of God the Father, but will soon come from heaven to claim His bride, the church.

Holy Spirit – Third person of the Godhead. When Jesus ascended to heaven, He sent down the

Holy Spirit - As believers, He dwells in us leading, guiding, revealing, strengthening, and healing.

CHAPTER 1
QUESTIONS AND ANSWERS

1.   All of creation, including mankind was drastically and negatively transformed by just one thing, the _sin_ of Adam.

2.   _Original sin_ is a description of the universal condition and consequence of man's sin that all of creation remains under.

3.   When looking at His creation, God saw that all of it was _good_

4.   The bible says that _all_ have sinned and fallen short of God's glory.

5.   The Greek word for 'saved' is _sozo_ which means _to save, heal, cure, preserve, keep safe, deliver, etc_

6.   Jesus was born of a _virgin_ and lived a _sinless_ life.

7.   God put _own sins_ on Jesus on the cross and His _righteousness_ me.

8.   Because God is _omniscient_ He has _foreknowledge_ and knew even before the beginning of creation that man would fall into sin.

9.   Because Jesus said yes to the Father before creation, the bible calls Him the _Lamb slain_ from the foundation of the world in Revelation 13:8

10. In Ephesians 2:8 the bible tells us we're saved by _grace_ through _faith_

11. Salvation is God's _free gift_ and it is for _all_ mankind.

12. As a believer, you cannot nor do you have the need to ever being
saved again.

13. As a Christian, when you sin God does not _dison_ you, _reject_
you or _give_ _up_ on you.

14. The _grace_ He has for us will always be more and greater than the
sin we bring to Him.

15. _grace_ never loses a battle to _sin_.

16. When we're quick to admit ~~we're sinners~~ _we are wrong_, He's quick to
~~restore~~ _forgive us_ and make us ~~clean~~ _strong_

17. No one can take your _salvation_ from you.

18. Salvation is not the _end_, but rather, the _beginning_ of the
glorious things He has for you.

19. The _bible_ is your map and the _Holy_ _Spirit_ is your
guide in this lifelong adventure of pursuing and discovering God and His glorious grace.

2 JESUS CHRIST OUR BAPTIZER

WATER BAPTISM

Accepting Jesus Christ as Savior is an internal act of our hearts through believing. All believers are then instructed by the Word of God to continue following Christ in the external act of water baptism. Water baptism was taught and practiced by the early church as a necessary and vital element of commitment, devotion and discipleship for all who would become believers. Water baptism without believing in the saving work and Lordship of Jesus Christ is an empty, meaningless religious gesture. Baptism without belief cannot save anyone. But after a person repents (changes his or her mind) and believes that Jesus Christ died for their sins and through His shed blood gives us forgiveness and eternal life, then all believers are commanded to follow Christ in the act of being water baptized in the name of Jesus.

Jesus Himself is the originator of the commitment to be water baptized after believing.

Mark 16:15-16 (NKJV) reads:

> And He said to them, "Go into all the world and preach the gospel to every creature. He who believes and is baptized will be saved; but he who does not believe

will be condemned.

In the first sermon of the early church, the Apostle Peter invited the many thousands that he was preaching to, to receive salvation through repentance and then to be immediately baptized in water as a public acknowledgement of their faith in Christ.

> Acts 2:38, 40-41 (NKJV)
> Then Peter said to them, "Repent, and let every one of you be baptized in the name of Jesus Christ for the remission of sins; and you shall receive the gift of the Holy Spirit.
> And with many other words he testified and exhorted them, saying, "Be saved from this perverse generation." Then those who gladly received his word were baptized; and that day about three thousand souls were added to them.

In the mind, belief and practice of the early church repentance (changing our minds, believing in the saving grace of Jesus, turning from our sins) and water baptism were inseparably connected. Being in Christ meant to then be immediately baptized in water. The Bible records another example of this pattern in Acts 8:12 (NKJV):

> But when they believed Philip as he preached the things concerning the kingdom of God and the name of Jesus Christ, both men and women were baptized.

The sequence of hearing the good news of the gospel of Jesus Christ, to believe and to then be water baptized is shown perfectly in Acts 8:35-38 (NKJV):

> Then Philip opened his mouth, and beginning at this Scripture, preached Jesus to him. Now as they went down the road, they came to some water. And the eunuch said, "See, here is water. What hinders me from being baptized?"
> Then Philip said, "If you believe with all your heart, you may."
> And he answered and said, "I believe that Jesus Christ is the Son of God."
> So he commanded the chariot to stand still. And both Philip and the eunuch went down into the water, and he baptized him.

The practice of water baptism is seen throughout the growth of the early church as people were coming to Christ in salvation.

Acts 10:47-48 (NKJV)

"Can anyone forbid water, that these should not be baptized who have received the Holy Spirit just as we have?" And he commanded them to be baptized in the name of the Lord. Then they asked him to stay a few days.

Acts 16:15 (NKJV)

And when she and her household were baptized, she begged us, saying, "If you have judged me to be faithful to the Lord, come to my house and stay." So she persuaded us.

Acts 16:31-33 (NKJV)

So they said, "Believe on the Lord Jesus Christ, and you will be saved, you and your household." Then they spoke the word of the Lord to him and to all who were in his house. And he took them the same hour of the night and washed their stripes. And immediately he and all his family were baptized.

Acts 18:8 (NKJV)

Then Crispus, the ruler of the synagogue, believed on the Lord with all his household. And many of the Corinthians, hearing, believed and were baptized.

Acts 22:16 (NKJV)

And now why are you waiting? Arise and be baptized, and wash away your sins, calling on the name of the Lord.'

Beyond being a public acknowledgement of our faith in Jesus Christ, what is the spiritual significance and meaning of water baptism?

Romans 6:3-5 (MSG) reads:

That is what happened in baptism. When we went under the water, we left the old country of sin behind; when we came up out of the water, we entered into the new country of grace—a new life in a new land!

That's what baptism into the life of Jesus means. When we are lowered into the water, it is like the burial of Jesus; when we are raised up out of the water, it is like the resurrection of Jesus. Each of us is raised into a light-filled world by our Father so that we can see where we're going in our new grace-sovereign country.

In water baptism we are personally identifying with the death, burial and resurrection of Jesus Christ. Water baptism is much more than just a religious ritual or church tradition. Instead, it is a powerful spiritual experience where our lives are dynamically ministered to. When we are baptized under water, at that moment we are identifying with the death and burial of Christ. Our 'old' life is buried in the water forever.

When the children of Israel came out of Egypt (Egypt is a type of the world) they were miraculously delivered through the 'passover' where each Jewish household marked its doorposts with the blood of a blemishless lamb. The lamb is a symbol of Jesus Christ who is called "the Lamb of God which takes away the sin of the world" in John 1:29. Each Jewish household was 'saved' by the blood of the lamb just as we as believers are saved by the precious blood of our Savior Jesus Christ. After the Passover all of the Jews were released by Pharoah from over 400 years of slavery in Egypt. As they marched out of Egypt they came to the Red Sea where God opened the waters and they all walked across the dry seabed to the other side. As they were finishing their journey crossing the Red Sea, Pharoah and the Egyptians changed their minds about releasing the Jews. Pharoah (whose name means 'spoiler king' is a type of the enemy of mankind, Satan) led his army into the parted Red Sea in order to recapture their former slaves, the Hebrews. When Pharoah and his mighty army had entered into the Red Sea, suddenly God brought down the great walls of water on each side of them. They were all destroyed in the waters of the Red Sea. This is an awesome portrait of what happens in the life of believers when they're baptized in water. God delivers us from the power of our past to ever control and oppress us ever again! All the forces and strongholds that enslaved and controlled us before we were believers are broken off of us in water baptism. The power of the devil is 'drowned' in the waters of baptism. The power that the world once had over us is 'drowned' in the waters of baptism as we experience victory our Savior has won for us. (The story of the deliverance of the Jews from Egypt is found in the book of Exodus).

We not only by faith identify with and experience the death and burial of Christ through baptism, when we are raised up out of water, we then follow Christ in His joyous resurrection from the dead into new life. These Scriptures describe what happens in our lives:

I Peter 3:21 (MSG)
The waters of baptism do that for you, not by washing away dirt from your skin but by presenting you through Jesus' resurrection before God with a clear conscience.

Galatians 3:27 (MSG)
Your baptism in Christ was not just washing you up for a fresh start. It also involved dressing you in an adult faith wardrobe—Christ's life, the fulfillment of God's original promise.

Colossians 2:12 (MSG)
Going under the water was a burial of your old life; coming up out of it was a resurrection, God raising you from the dead as he did Christ.

Water baptism is the place where our faith is engaged to receive what Christ has done for us. As we're submerged in water, all of our old life is submerged into the ocean of God's love for us. We are acknowledging and accepting the death of Christ to be in our place, for our sins. We are accepting the truth that He took our place on the cross and died when our sins were put on Him by God. Our old life is now 'deceased' with Him. It has no more control over who we are and what we do. As good as all that is, the greatest part of the cross was not our Savior's death, but His glorious resurrection from the dead. So it is in baptism, the greatest grace that floods into our lives as we follow Christ in water baptism is not being delivered from our past, but the more superior blessing is that just as He was raised up from death, so when we are raised up out of the water we have been given the resurrection life of Christ Himself! We are raised in newness of life, a life we've never known before and a life that is eternal and abundant! We have been baptized into the very life and nature of Jesus Christ Himself. This life is now our life.

CHAPTER 2
QUESTIONS AND ANSWERS

1. Water baptism with belief in the _death_ _burial and resurrection_ _of_ _Jesus_ _Christ_ is an _____ _____ _____ _____.

2. In Mark 16:15-16 the Bible tells us that _____ _____ is the origination of the commandment to be water baptized after believing.

3. In Acts 2:38 the Apostle Peter, in the first sermon of the early church, invited all those who heard him to _repent_ and be _baptized_

4. In the _mind_, _belief_ and _practice_ of the early church repentance and baptism were inseparably connected.

5. In Acts 8:35-38 we see the sequence of actions. First it is in _hearing_ the goodness of the gospel, then those who hear _believe_ and after believing they were _baptized_

6. In the book of Exodus, the destruction of Pharoah and his army in the _Red Sea_ is a type of what _____ _____ does for us as believers.

7. The forces and strongholds that enslaved and controlled us before we were believers are broken off of us in _water_ _baptism_

8. Just as Jesus was raised up from death, when we are raised up out of the water in baptism, we've been given _the_ _resurrection_ _Jesus_ _Christ_ _life_

3 THE BAPTISM OF THE HOLY SPIRIT

Jesus Christ is our Baptizer. He is the one we are baptized in water into. He is the one who promised and then provided the next baptism, the baptism of the Holy Spirit. Jesus promised He would send the Holy Spirit to us.

John 14:16-17 (NKJV)
And I will pray the Father, and He will give you another Helper, that He may abide with you forever— the Spirit of truth, whom the world cannot receive, because it neither sees Him nor knows Him; but you know Him, for He dwells with you and will be in you.

John 16:7-15 (NKJV)
Nevertheless I tell you the truth. It is to your advantage that I go away; for if I do not go away, the Helper will not come to you; but if I depart, I will send Him to you. And when He has come, He will convict the world of sin, and of righteousness, and of judgment: of sin, because they do not believe in Me; of righteousness, because I go to My Father and you see Me no more; of judgment, because the ruler of this world is judged. "I still have many things to say to you, but you cannot bear them now. However, when He, the Spirit of truth, has come, He will guide you

into all truth; for He will not speak on His own authority, but whatever He hears He will speak; and He will tell you things to come. He will glorify Me, for He will take of what is Mine and declare it to you. All things that the Father has are Mine. Therefore I said that He will take of Mine and declare it to you.

John 14:26 (NKJV)
But the Helper, the Holy Spirit, whom the Father will send in My name, He will teach you all things, and bring to your remembrance all things that I said to you.

WHAT IS THE BAPTISM OF THE HOLY SPIRIT?

Let's begin by understanding who the Holy Spirit is:

• He is the third person in the Godhead. The Holy Spirit is not an 'experience' or 'gift.' He is a person and He is God. The Holy Spirit possesses all the divine attributes of God. He is omnipotent (all-powerful). (Luke 1:35) He is omniscient (all-knowing). (I Cor. 2:10, 11) He is omnipresent. (Ps. 139:7-10)

• The Holy Spirit is a person and possesses the attributes of mind (Rom. 8:27), will (I Cor. 12:11) and emotion (Eph. 4:30).

As such, when we are 'baptized' in the Holy Spirit, we are 'filled' or 'immersed' into the life and attributes of the person and God He is. To be baptized in the Holy Spirit is to have our lives flooded with the gifts, graces and glory that He possesses. It means to acknowledge and receive His superior abilities and to surrender our weaknesses to His strength. The Bible commands believers to be filled with the Spirit.

Ephesians 5:18 (NKJV)
And do not be drunk with wine, in which is dissipation; but be filled with the Spirit...

We have in the narrative of the scripture an example and guide to receive the Holy Spirit's baptism. Jesus told the disciples to wait for the promise of the Holy Spirit in Luke 24:49 (NKJV):

"Behold, I send the Promise of My Father upon you; but tarry in the city of Jerusalem until you are endued with power from on high."

In Acts chapter two we have the fulfillment of the promise of the Holy Spirit to the early church.

Acts 2:1-17 (NKJV)

When the Day of Pentecost had fully come, they were all with one accord in one place.

And suddenly there came a sound from heaven, as of a rushing mighty wind, and it filled the whole house where they were sitting. Then there appeared to them divided tongues, as of fire, and one sat upon each of them. And they were all filled with the Holy Spirit and began to speak with other tongues, as the Spirit gave them utterance.

And there were dwelling in Jerusalem Jews, devout men, from every nation under heaven. And when this sound occurred, the multitude came together, and were confused, because everyone heard them speak in his own language. Then they were all amazed and marveled, saying to one another, "Look, are not all these who speak Galileans? And how is it that we hear, each in our own language in which we were born? Parthians and Medes and Elamites, those dwelling in Mesopotamia, Judea and Cappadocia, Pontus and Asia, Phrygia and Pamphylia, Egypt and the parts of Libya adjoining Cyrene, visitors from Rome, both Jews and proselytes,   Cretans and Arabs—we hear them speaking in our own tongues the wonderful works of God." So they were all amazed and perplexed, saying to one another, "Whatever could this mean?"

Others mocking said, "They are full of new wine."

But Peter, standing up with the eleven, raised his voice and said to them, "Men of Judea and all who dwell in Jerusalem, let this be known to you, and heed my words. For these are not drunk, as you suppose, since it is only the third hour of the day. But this is what was spoken by the prophet Joel: 'And it shall come to pass in the last days, says God, that I will pour out of My Spirit on all flesh; your sons and your daughters shall prophesy, your young men shall see visions, your old men shall dream dreams.

The Apostle Peter gave the 'altar call' after prophesying the message in Acts 2:38-39 (NKJV):

> Then Peter said to them, "Repent, and let every one of you be baptized in the name of Jesus Christ for the remission of sins; and you shall receive the gift of the Holy Spirit. For the promise is to you and to your children, and to all who are afar off, as many as the Lord our God will call."

Notice the sequence in Scripture:
1. Repentance (turn from sin, receiving forgiveness and new life through Jesus Christ)
2. Be water baptized
3. Receive the gift of the Holy Spirit (Baptism of the Holy Spirit)

A great crowd of people had gathered around the 120 disciples who had been gloriously Spirit-filled. The interest of the people was in the expression of speaking in other tongues that was happening to the newly Spirit-baptized church. Peter made it clear; they could all receive the same baptism or filling of the Holy Spirit as the 120 had just received. The steps were simple then and they remain uncomplicated now. Step one: Repent from sin and receive the gift of salvation by faith in Jesus Christ. Anyone could be saved then, and so you can receive God's free gift of salvation now. Step two: Be baptized in water as a public act of faith in Christ, identifying with His death and burial, and receiving the new life He gives to all who come to Him. Step three: Ask for and then receive the Gift of the Holy Spirit Baptism in your life. As Peter said, "For the promise (of the Gift of the Holy Spirit) is to you and to your children, and to all who are afar off, as many as the Lord our God will call."

It is imperative that you clearly see that the Scriptures teach the infilling of the Holy Spirit (baptism) as a separate and unique experience from both initial salvation, and then water baptism. Holy Spirit baptism comes after salvation and is available to every believer. These scriptures make this absolutely clear for us.

Acts 8:14-17 (NKJV)
Now when the apostles who were at Jerusalem heard that Samaria had received the

word of God, they sent Peter and John to them, who, when they had come down, prayed for them that they might receive the Holy Spirit. For as yet He had fallen upon none of them. They had only been baptized in the name of the Lord Jesus. Then they laid hands on them, and they received the Holy Spirit.

Acts 19:1-6 (NKJV)
And it happened, while Apollos was at Corinth, that Paul, having passed through the upper regions, came to Ephesus. And finding some disciples he said to them, "Did you receive the Holy Spirit when you believed?"

So they said to him, "We have not so much as heard whether there is a Holy Spirit."

And he said to them, "Into what then were you baptized?"
So they said, "Into John's baptism."

Then Paul said, "John indeed baptized with a baptism of repentance, saying to the people that they should believe on Him who would come after him, that is, on Christ Jesus."

When they heard this, they were baptized in the name of the Lord Jesus. And when Paul had laid hands on them, the Holy Spirit came upon them, and they spoke with tongues and prophesied.

Acts 10:44-48 (NKJV)
While Peter was still speaking these words, the Holy Spirit fell upon all those who heard the word. And those of the circumcision who believed were astonished, as many as came with Peter, because the gift of the Holy Spirit had been poured out on the Gentiles also. For they heard them speak with tongues and magnify God.

Then Peter answered, "Can anyone forbid water, that these should not be baptized who have received the Holy Spirit just as we have?" And he commanded them to be baptized in the name of the Lord. Then they asked him to stay a few days.

In this passage we see the Holy Spirit gloriously falling for the first time upon gentile (non-Jewish) believers. They received the Baptism of the Holy Spirit before they'd ever been water Baptized. The Apostle recognized what God had done and soon had them all be water baptized also. The importance is not that the two types of baptism happened out of normal order, but that there were two baptisms for them to experience.

Do I have to speak in tongues in order to be filled with the Holy Spirit?

Let's look at the pattern of speaking in tongues in the book of Acts. When the early believers received the baptism of the Holy Spirit, there was the initial evidence and manifestation of speaking in tongues in their lives.

> Acts 2:4 (NKJV)
> And they were all filled with the Holy Spirit and began to speak with other tongues, as the Spirit gave them utterance.

> Acts 10:46(a) (NKJV)
> For they heard them speak with tongues and magnify God.

> Acts 19:6 (NKJV)
> And when Paul had laid hands on them, the Holy Spirit came upon them, and they spoke with tongues and prophesied.

So if the biblical pattern for receiving the baptism of the Holy Spirit always includes the initial evidence of speaking in unknown tongues, why would we look for or accept anything less than what God gave them? While it may be possible to be Spirit baptized and not yet speak with other tongues, there should never be in that persons' life the acceptance that he or she never will receive the gift of tongues. I like to tell people that just like their shoes have a 'tongue' on them, that is a vital part of what the shoe is. And if you took the 'tongue' off the shoe, you might still have a shoe, but it would be incomplete and inferior to what it was designed to be. So it is with the gift of speaking in unknown tongues and the baptism of the Holy Spirit. Why would you not want all the gift and its tremendous benefit in your life?

The Bible gives us a rich revelation on the tremendous benefit and blessing that speaking in tongues brings to our lives as believers. Speaking in tongues edifies the believer.

> I Corinthians 14:1-5 (MSG)

Go after a life of love as if your life depended on it—because it does. Give yourselves to the gifts God gives you. Most of all, try to proclaim his truth. If you praise him in the private language of tongues, God understands you but no one else does, for you are sharing intimacies just between you and him. But when you proclaim his truth in everyday speech, you're letting others in on the truth so that they can grow and be strong and experience his presence with you.

The one who prays using a private "prayer language" certainly gets a lot out of it, but proclaiming God's truth to the church in its common language brings the whole church into growth and strength. I want all of you to develop intimacies with God in prayer, but please don't stop with that. Go on and proclaim his clear truth to others. It's more important that everyone have access to the knowledge and love of God in language everyone understands than that you go off and cultivate God's presence in a mysterious prayer language—unless, of course, there is someone who can interpret what you are saying for the benefit of all.

I Corinthians 14:15 (NKJV)
What is the conclusion then? I will pray with the spirit, and I will also pray with the understanding. I will sing with the spirit, and I will also sing with the understanding.

I Corinthians 14:18 (NKJV)
I thank my God I speak with tongues more than you all;

I Corinthians 14:39 (NKJV)
Therefore, brethren, desire earnestly to prophesy, and do not forbid to speak with tongues.

Jude 20 (NKJV)
But you, beloved, building yourselves up on your most holy faith, praying in the Holy Spirit...

Speaking in tongues brings personal edification to the person doing it. It builds their faith and makes them strong. When it is interpreted, it is a powerful gift for the public assembly of the church.

Speaking in tongues is also a beautiful way of expressing a deeper and greater worship to God from our spirit. When we 'sing in tongues,' it is a spiritual song that ministers to God.

I Corinthians 14:15 (NKJV)
What is the conclusion then? I will pray with the spirit, and I will also pray with the understanding. I will sing with the spirit, and I will also sing with the understanding.

Ephesians 5:18-19 (NKJV)
And do not be drunk with wine, in which is dissipation; but be filled with the Spirit,
speaking to one another in psalms and hymns and spiritual songs, singing and making melody in your heart to the Lord...

One of the most valuable functions of speaking in tongues is in the place of Spirit-led intercession.

Romans 8:26 (NKJV)
Likewise the Spirit also helps in our weaknesses. For we do not know what we should pray for as we ought, but the Spirit Himself makes intercession for us with groanings which cannot be uttered.

Ephesians 6:18 (NKJV)
...praying always with all prayer and supplication in the Spirit, being watchful to this
end with all perseverance and supplication for all the saints

I Corinthians 14:14 (NKJV)
For if I pray in a tongue, my spirit prays, but my understanding is unfruitful.

Think about this: when we pray in tongues, it is not 'our' mind directing the words, but the 'mind of the Spirit' is being expressed in the tongues He prays through us. That means that at that moment we're praying the most perfect prayer imaginable, because it is God's mind and words, not ours that is flowing from us. The omniscience (all-knowing) of God is now expressing itself in a prayer that is exactly perfect for the situation. When we intercede in tongues, it is a prayer that will always 'hit the mark' of expressing God's perfect will on the matter. What a great blessing to know that we have this incredible gift of being able to break free from the limitations of our own ability, knowledge and mind, and can wonderfully access God's ability, knowledge and mind when we allow the Person of the Holy Spirit to pray through us with other tongues.

THE BAPTISM OF THE HOLY SPIRIT BRINGS HEAVEN'S POWER INTO OUR LIVES.

Acts 1:8 (NKJV)

"But you shall receive power when the Holy Spirit has come upon you; and you shall be witnesses to Me in Jerusalem, and in all Judea and Samaria, and to the end of the earth."

The Holy Spirit's presence in our lives makes available supernatural strength and power. When we are filled with the Holy Spirit with the evidence of speaking in tongues, we are connected to the glorious river of spiritual gifts and abilities He brings.

Jesus said in John 7:37-39 (NKJV, MSG):

On the last day, that great day of the feast, Jesus stood and cried out, saying, "If anyone thirsts, let him come to Me and drink. He who believes in Me, as the Scripture has said, out of his heart will flow rivers of living water." But this He spoke concerning the Spirit, whom those believing in Him would receive; for the Holy Spirit was not yet given, because Jesus was not yet glorified.

On the final and climactic day of the Feast, Jesus took his stand. He cried out, "If anyone thirsts, let him come to me and drink. Rivers of living water will brim and spill out of the depths of anyone who believes in me this way, just as the Scripture says." (He said this in regard to the Spirit, whom those who believed in him were about to receive. The Spirit had not yet been given because Jesus had not yet been glorified.)

Here's a simple analogy I use about the tremendous importance of the gift of the Holy Spirit in our lives. When a person accepts Christ as Savior, the Bible says they are made a new creation: I use the example of a brand new car, no repairs needed, no damage done, everything in perfect working order. The baptism of the Holy Spirit is like the gasoline needed for the car to run at full capacity. When our lives (cars) have the infilling of the Holy Spirit (gasoline) we then experience all the capacity that is available. Some believers are like a brand new car, but instead of going places and doing great things for God, they remain 'parked,' because they haven't received the power the Holy Spirit brings.

Jesus, Himself, preached no sermon, performed no miracle, healed no broken life until He was baptized in the Holy Spirit at the age of 30.

Matthew 3:16 (NKJV) reads:

> When He had been baptized, Jesus came up immediately from the water; and behold, the heavens were opened to Him, and He saw the Spirit of God descending like a dove and alighting upon Him.

Jesus did not minister in His earthly ministry under the privileges of His divine right and attributes as God. When He was incarnate (took physical form and the Word became flesh) He emptied Himself of all His Divine capacities.

> Philippians 2:5-8 (NKJV)
> Let this mind be in you which was also in Christ Jesus, who, being in the form of God, did not consider it robbery to be equal with God, but made Himself of no reputation, taking the form of a bondservant, and coming in the likeness of men. And being found in appearance as a man, He humbled Himself and became obedient to the point of death, even the death of the cross.

Every miracle He did, He did under the control and capacity of the Holy Spirit. That's why He's commanded us to replicate His works in our lives and ministries. Because we have the same Holy Spirit that He was filled with.

John 14:12 (NKJV)

"Most assuredly, I say to you, he who believes in Me, the works that I do he will do also and greater works than these he will do, because I go to My Father.

Jesus exemplified what it means to be Spirit-filled, Spirit-led and Spirit-empowered. What He did we can do also by being Holy Spirit filled, led and empowered as believers.

Through the baptism of the Holy Spirit the believer has access to flow and function in the gifts of the Holy Spirit.

I Corinthians 12:1, 7-11 (NKJV)

Now concerning spiritual gifts, brethren, I do not want you to be ignorant: But the manifestation of the Spirit is given to each one for the profit of all: for to one is given the word of wisdom through the Spirit, to another the word of knowledge through the same Spirit, to another faith by the same Spirit, to another gifts of healings by the same Spirit, to another the working of miracles, to another prophecy, to another discerning of spirits, to another different kinds of tongues, to another the interpretation of tongues. But one and the same Spirit works all these things, distributing to each one individually as He wills.

Here is a brief description of the 9 Gifts of the Holy Spirit. We'll divide the nine gifts into three categories.

I. THE UTTERANCE GIFTS – (GIFTS SPOKEN)

Prophecy: A divinely inspired utterance that brings edification, encouragement and healing to others. It is a manifestation of the Holy Spirit - not of human intellect. All believers who are filled with the Holy Spirit may seek to be used in the gifts of prophecy. In I Cor. 14:1 we are told to passionately desire the gift of prophecy.

Diverse Tongues: The spiritual gift of tongues listed in I Cor. 12 is when unknown tongues are spoken at the direction of the Holy Spirit for the precise purpose of then being immediately interpreted into a known language. It is a different kind of tongue than a normal unknown tongue prayer language.

Interpretation of Tongues: After a 'message' in different tongues, the Holy Spirit then anoints someone (usually the same person who gave the diverse tongue) to reveal the meaning of the tongue. It is not the operation of human intellect or ability, but the work of the Holy Spirit.

II. THE REVELATION GIFTS

Word of Knowledge: God is omniscient (all-knowing) and with this gift the Holy Spirit reveals knowledge we could not have accessed without Him. It is a fragment of God's omniscience without human assistance used to bring healing, deliverance, guidance, protection, and provision into peoples lives.

Word of Wisdom: The gift of the word of wisdom is when the Holy Spirit gives us supernatural insight to accomplish the will of God. It is a divine anointing to solve problems by accessing God's specific wisdom for what is needed. This gift makes known God's will through revealing direction for right decisions.

Discerning of Spirits: Supernatural revelation into the true nature of the spiritual activity in people or situations. Insight into spiritual reality through discerning presence of angels, demons, or God's presence. Discovering the spirit that is operating in a person's life.

III. THE POWER GIFTS

Working of Miracles: The gift of working of miracles is when the Holy Spirit overcomes natural law in order to supernaturally bring about God's will - something that could otherwise not be accomplished without the manifestation of the miraculous ability of God. God, by nature, possesses miraculous qualities and He reveals His personal nature through miracles to those in need.

Gifts of Healing: Gifts (plural) of healing are the work of supernatural healing without human assistance. There are many different uses of this gift as some people have this gift concerning a specific area of healing. People who flow in this gift see great results when praying for someone they have the gift of healing for their disease.

Gift of (Supernatural) Faith: To possess in a certain moment the supernatural capacity to believe God without doubt. This gift works in partnership with the other gifts (miracles, healing) to accomplish God's will.

When a believer has been filled with the baptism of the Holy Spirit, the glorious world of these nine spiritual gifts is unconditionally opened to their exploration and experience. Just because a person is "spirit-filled" does not necessarily mean that these gifts will automatically begin flowing in their lives. We must, as the Bible says, "earnestly desire" the operation of these spiritual gifts in our lives. We must hunger and seek for the manifestation of the gifts of the Spirit in our lives. The Bible tells us that "all may prophesy" and that we should all "desire spiritual gifts, but especially that you may prophesy." Every believer is called to receive and express the gift of prophecy. You can have this gift in your life as a child of God, filled with the Holy Spirit.

THE FRUIT OF THE SPIRIT

Not only are these nine gifts of the Spirit revealed in God's Word, but there are also nine fruits of the Spirit. Picture with me a beautiful, great eagle that's soaring in the sky. With both of his wings fully extended this majestic creature moves effortlessly through the air. The eagle soars when both his wings are present, healthy and in operation. The believer's life soars when both wings are present and extended to catch the wind of the Holy Spirit and carry us to great heights in God. For us as believers, our wings are exemplified in the nine gifts of the Spirit (one wing) and the nine fruits of the Spirit (other wing). One wing without the other makes flight impossible. One wing open and one wing closed makes flight impossible. The nine fruits of the Spirit is the impartation of the character and nature of Christ to us as believers through the indwelling presence of the Holy Spirit. The nine gifts of the Holy Spirit are the operation of the mighty power of God entrusted to the believer through the Holy Spirit. The two wings are here. One is power through spiritual gifts. The other is Christ-like character through spiritual fruit. One is not more essential than the other. Neither is to be deemed insignificant or unessential for the life of the believer. Together they form God's will and God's best for what every believer should experience in this world following Christ.

Through the indwelling presence of the Holy Spirit in our lives, the fruit of the Spirit is in us, present through the Holy Spirit's abiding presence. The promises of God's Word reveal the splendor of God's grace that we have been called and qualified to inherit and experience as His children. The Bible declares that the fruit of the Spirit is ours as Christians in Galatians 5:22-23 (NKJV):

> But the fruit of the Spirit is love, joy, peace, longsuffering, kindness, goodness, faithfulness, gentleness, self-control. Against such there is no law.

Every day in my personal prayer time, I thank the Holy Spirit for each one of these nine fruits in my life. I claim them and ask that I be filled and controlled by their presence in my life.

The Greek structure of these verses suggests there is one fruit with 9 different qualities. The fruit is love and the following eight virtues are different expressions of the working of love.

1. LOVE

The Greek word for love in the New Testament is 'agape.' This word was either invented or adopted by Christ in that it is unused in literature before His life and teaching. This is God's love, not human love. The Bible describes this love in I Corinthians 13:1-8 (NLT, MSG):

> If I could speak all the languages of earth and of angels, but didn't love others, I would only be a noisy gong or a clanging cymbal. If I had the gift of prophecy, and if I understood all of God's secret plans and possessed all knowledge, and if I had such faith that I could move mountains, but didn't love others, I would be nothing. If I gave everything I have to the poor and even sacrificed my body, I could boast about it; but if I didn't love others, I would have gained nothing. Love is patient and kind. Love is not jealous or boastful or proud or rude. It does not demand its own way. It is not irritable, and it keeps no record of being wronged. It does not rejoice about injustice but rejoices whenever the truth wins out. Love never gives up, never loses faith, is always hopeful, and endures through every circumstance.
>
> Prophecy and speaking in unknown languages and special knowledge will become useless. But love will last forever!

If I speak with human eloquence and angelic ecstasy but don't love, I'm nothing but the creaking of a rusty gate. If I speak God's Word with power, revealing all his mysteries and making everything plain as day, and if I have faith that says to a mountain, "Jump," and it jumps, but I don't love, I'm nothing. If I give everything I own to the poor and even go to the stake to be burned as a martyr, but I don't love, I've gotten nowhere. So, no matter what I say, what I believe, and what I do, I'm bankrupt without love.

Love never gives up. Love cares more for others than for self. Love doesn't want what it doesn't have. Love doesn't strut, doesn't have a swelled head, doesn't force itself on others, isn't always "me first," doesn't fly off the handle, doesn't keep score of the sins of others, doesn't revel when others grovel, takes pleasure in the flowering of truth, puts up with anything, trusts God always, always looks for the best, never looks back, but keeps going to the end.

Love never dies. Inspired speech will be over some day; praying in tongues will end; understanding will reach its limit.

As believers indwelt by the Holy Spirit, we are all filled with God's love as this verse describes.

Romans 5:5 (NKJV) says:

Now hope does not disappoint, because the love of God has been poured out in our hearts by the Holy Spirit who was given to us.

Jesus said that the unsaved world around us would know we're His disciples through our love for each other.

John 13:34-35 (NKJV)
"A new commandment I give to you, that you love one another; as I have loved you, that you also love one another. By this all will know that you are My disciples, if you have love for one another."

Love is the very nature of God Himself.

I John 4:16 (NKJV)

And we have known and believed the love that God has for us. God is love, and he who abides in love abides in God, and God in him.

When we live our lives filled with God's love for others, we are Christ-like and God-pleasing.

I John 4:7-8 (NKJV, MSG)

Beloved, let us love one another, for love is of God; and everyone who loves is born of God and knows God. He who does not love does not know God, for God is love.

My beloved friends, let us continue to love each other since love comes from God. Everyone who loves is born of God and experiences a relationship with God. The person who refuses to love doesn't know the first thing about God, because God is love—so you can't know him if you don't love.

2. JOY

The presence of the Holy Spirit in our lives gives us unconditional access to heavenly joy in this lifetime. It's God's will for you to be happy!

John 15:11 (NKJV, AMP)

"These things I have spoken to you, that My joy may remain in you, and that your joy may be full.

I have told you these things, that My joy and delight may be in you, and that your joy and gladness may be of full measure and complete and overflowing.

John 16:22, 24 (NKJV, AMP)

Therefore you now have sorrow; but I will see you again and your heart will rejoice, and your joy no one will take from you.

Until now you have asked nothing in My name. Ask, and you will receive, that your joy may be full.

So for the present you are also in sorrow (in distress and depressed); but I will see you again and [then] your hearts will rejoice, and no one can take from you your joy (gladness, delight).

> Up to this time you have not asked a [single] thing in My Name [as presenting all that I AM]; but now ask and keep on asking and you will receive, so that your joy (gladness, delight) may be full and complete.

The Holy Spirit is the earthly governor of the Kingdom of God. His presence in our lives grants us unconditional access to joy.

> Romans 14:17 (NKJV)
> ...for the kingdom of God is not eating and drinking, but righteousness and peace and joy in the Holy Spirit.

Joy for the Holy Spirit believer does not happen by chance, but joy is our choice!

3. PEACE

The Hebrew word for peace is 'Shalom' which means "completeness, wholeness, health, safety, soundness, prosperity, perfectness, fullness, rest, harmony. To have nothing missing or lacking." What an awesome blessing God has given us in this peace! Peace is yours!

> Romans 14:17 (NKJV)
> ...for the kingdom of God is not eating and drinking, but righteousness and peace and joy in the Holy Spirit.

Jesus said He was giving us this peace in John 14:27 (NKJV, NLT):

> Peace I leave with you, My peace I give to you; not as the world gives do I give to you. Let not your heart be troubled, neither let it be afraid.

> "I am leaving you with a gift—peace of mind and heart. And the peace I give is a gift the world cannot give. So don't be troubled or afraid."

The peace of God is more powerful than anything in this world.

> Colossians 3:15 (NKJV)

And let the peace of God rule in your hearts, to which also you were called in one body; and be thankful.

By giving our problems and burdens to God in prayer, we can habitually abide under the presence and protection of this wonderful peace.

Philippians 4:6-7 (NKJV)
Be anxious for nothing, but in everything by prayer and supplication, with thanksgiving, let your requests be made known to God; and the peace of God, which surpasses all understanding, will guard your hearts and minds through Christ Jesus.

Isaiah 26:3 (NKJV)
You will keep him in perfect peace, whose mind is stayed on You, because he trusts in You.

4. PATIENCE/LONGSUFFERING

The Greek word used in Galatians 5:22 for longsuffering is 'makrothumia' which means "fortitude, patent endurance, forbearance, the ability to endure persecution and ill-treatment. The ability to use restraint when having the power to exercise revenge." We are told in Scripture to put on this blessed virtue.

Colossians 3:12 (NKJV)
Therefore, as the elect of God, holy and beloved, put on tender mercies, kindness, humility, meekness, longsuffering;

Hebrews 12:1 (NKJV)
Therefore we also, since we are surrounded by so great a cloud of witnesses, let us lay aside every weight, and the sin which so easily ensnares us, and let us run with endurance the race that is set before us,

The great benefit of longsuffering to us is told in Hebrews 6:12 (NKJV):

... that you do not become sluggish, but imitate those who through faith and patience inherit the promises.

5. KINDNESS

God is kind to all mankind. His children are to display the same kindness through their lives to other people.

> Luke 6:35(b) (NKJV)
> But love your enemies, do good, and lend, hoping for nothing in return...

> Isaiah 54:8 (NKJV)
> With a little wrath I hid My face from you for a moment; but with everlasting kindness I will have mercy on you," says the LORD, your Redeemer.

> Ephesians 4:32 (NKJV)
> And be kind to one another, tenderhearted, forgiving one another, even as God in Christ forgave you.

Small acts of kindness done with great love, will change the world, one good deed at a time.

6. GOODNESS

God is good. His goodness is overflowing in our lives as believers. His goodness is also to flow out of our lives to others.

> Psalm 23:6 (NKJV)
> Surely goodness and mercy shall follow me all the days of my life; and I will dwell in the house of the LORD forever.

> Psalm 33:5 (NKJV)
> He loves righteousness and justice; the earth is full of the goodness of the LORD.

> Psalm 100:5 (NKJV)
> For the LORD is good; His mercy is everlasting, and His truth endures to all generations.

Ephesians 5:9 (NKJV)

...(for the fruit of the Spirit is in all goodness, righteousness, and truth),

7. FAITHFULNESS

God is faithful and through the Holy Spirit's fruit in our lives we can experience this important virtue.

Lamentations 3:23 (NKJV)

They are new every morning; great is Your faithfulness.

I Thessalonians 5:24 (NKJV)

He who calls you is faithful, who also will do it.

I Corinthians 1:9 (NKJV)

God is faithful, by whom you were called into the fellowship of His Son, Jesus Christ our Lord.

Matthew 25:21 (NKJV)

His lord said to him, 'Well done, good and faithful servant; you were faithful over a few things, I will make you ruler over many things. Enter into the joy of your lord.'

Luke 16:10-11 (NKJV)

He who is faithful in what is least is faithful also in much; and he who is unjust in what is least is unjust also in much. Therefore if you have not been faithful in the unrighteous mammon, who will commit to your trust the true riches?

8. MEEKNESS/GENTLENESS

This is the Greek word 'praotes' which means "to be even-tempered, tranquil, balanced in spirit, unpretentious, having passions under control, meekness, strength under

control." Meekness is not weakness, but strength under control. Meekness brings God's blessings to our lives.

Matthew 5:5 (NKJV)

Blessed are the meek, for they shall inherit the earth.

Psalm 37:11 (NKJV)

But the meek shall inherit the earth, and shall delight themselves in the abundance of peace.

Psalm 147:6 (NKJV)

The LORD lifts up the humble; He casts the wicked down to the ground.

I Timothy 6:11 (NKJV)

But you, O man of God, flee these things and pursue righteousness, godliness, faith, love, patience, gentleness.

Titus 3:2 (NKJV)

...to speak evil of no one, to be peaceable, gentle, showing all humility to all men.

James 1:21 (NKJV)

Therefore lay aside all filthiness and overflow of wickedness, and receive with meekness the implanted word, which is able to save your souls.

9. SELF-CONTROL

Through the presence of the Holy Spirit in our lives we have a grace to govern with godliness our fleshly appetites and desires.

II Peter 1:5-8 (NKJV, MSG)

But also for this very reason, giving all diligence, add to your faith
virtue, to virtue knowledge, to knowledge self-control, to self-control perseverance, to perseverance godliness, to godliness brotherly kindness, and to brotherly kindness love. For if these things are yours and abound, you will be neither barren nor unfruitful in the knowledge of our Lord Jesus Christ.
So don't lose a minute in building on what you've been given, complementing your basic faith with good character, spiritual understanding, alert discipline, passionate patience, reverent wonder, warm friendliness, and generous love, each dimension

fitting into and developing the others. With these qualities active and growing in your lives, no grass will grow under your feet, no day will pass without its reward as you mature in your experience of our Master Jesus.

I John 4:4 (NKJV)
You are of God, little children, and have overcome them, because He who is in you is greater than he who is in the world.

Philippians 4:13 (NKJV)
I can do all things through Christ who strengthens me.

Have you received the baptism of the Holy Spirit with the scriptural evidence of speaking in other tongues? If not, then why not? Today's the day to receive this incredible gift that will radically transform your life. You don't have to be afraid to ask. Jesus said:

Luke 11:9-13 (NKJV)
"So I say to you, ask, and it will be given to you; seek, and you will find; knock, and it will be opened to you. For everyone who asks receives, and he who seeks finds, and to him who knocks it will be opened. If a son asks for bread from any father among you, will he give him a stone? Or if he asks for a fish, will he give him a serpent instead of a fish? Or if he asks for an egg, will he offer him a scorpion? If you then, being evil, know how to give good gifts to your children, how much more will your heavenly Father give the Holy Spirit to those who ask Him!"

Pray this prayer if you're ready to receive the baptism of the Holy Spirit:

"Father God, I thank you for the gift of salvation through the blood of your Son, Jesus Christ. I thank you for the promise to all believers of the gift of the Holy Spirit with the evidence of speaking in unknown tongues. I boldly now ask for this precious gift in the name of Jesus Christ. Amen."

After praying this prayer, remain in the spirit of faith and anticipation and expectancy. Keep your thoughts on this promised blessing being given to you. Know that He has heard and answered your sincere prayer. Begin by faith to allow the river of the Holy Spirit to flow through you with the gift of speaking in tongues. Let that heavenly language pour out of your spirit. Thank God for the incredible blessing and be sure to use your prayer language every day in prayer and worship.

CHAPTER 3
QUESTIONS AND ANSWERS

1. Jesus Christ is our _____.

2. The Holy Spirit is a _____ and possesses the attributes of _____ , _____ and _____.

3. In Acts 2:38-39 the three-fold sequence to receiving the baptism of the Holy Spirit was:

a._____

b._____

c._____

4. It is imperative you clearly see that the scriptures teach the infilling of the Holy Spirit (baptism) as a _____ and _____ _____ from both salvation and water baptism.

5. The biblical pattern for receiving the baptism of the Holy Spirit always includes the initial evidence of _____ ____ _____ _____.

6. Speaking in tongues brings _____ _____.

7. List the 9 Gifts of the Holy Spirit:

_____ , _____ , _____ ,
_____ , _____ , _____ ,
_____ , _____ , _____ .

8. List the 9 Fruits of the Spirit:

_____ , _____ , _____ ,
_____ , _____ , _____ ,
_____ , _____ , _____ .

9. The Bible says in Luke 11:13, "If you then, being evil, know how to give good gifts to your children, how much more will your heavenly Father give the _____ _____ to those who _____ _____."

4 JESUS CHRIST OUR HEALER

Jesus Christ is our Savior, Baptizer, and also our Healer. The grace of divine healing is available to mankind through the cross of Jesus Christ. Healing is as much a part of the finished work of the cross as salvation is (forgiveness of sins). God's incredible plan of Redemption through Jesus Christ includes the grace of healing for our mind, body and soul. In the most famous messianic prophecy in the Old Testament about what the Savior would accomplish for us, the Bible says:

Isaiah 53:3-5 (AMP)

"He was despised and rejected and forsaken by men, a Man of sorrows and pains, and acquainted with grief and sickness; and like One from Whom men hide their faces He was despised, and we did not appreciate His worth or have any esteem for Him. Surely He has borne our grief's (sicknesses, weaknesses, and distresses) and carried our sorrows and pains [of punishment], yet we [ignorantly] considered Him stricken, smitten, and afflicted by God [as if with leprosy]. But He was wounded for our transgressions, He was bruised for our guilt and iniquities; the chastisement [needful to obtain] peace and well-being for us was upon Him, and with the stripes [that wounded] Him we are healed and made whole.

Not only did God the Father put the sin of the all mankind on His Son at the cross, but the Bible boldly declares "By His stripes we are healed." Jesus bore the sickness, disease and pain of all mankind at the cross! In Mark 2:1-12 (NKJV) Jesus healed a paralyzed man and he united the forgiveness of sins and physical healing into one work.

> And again He entered Capernaum after some days, and it was heard that He was in the house. Immediately many gathered together, so that there was no longer room to receive them, not even near the door. And He preached the word to them. Then they came to Him, bringing a paralytic who was carried by four men. And when they could not come near Him because of the crowd, they uncovered the roof where He was. So when they had broken through, they let down the bed on which the paralytic was lying.
>
> When Jesus saw their faith, He said to the paralytic, "Son, your sins are forgiven you."
>
> And some of the scribes were sitting there and reasoning in their hearts, "Why does this Man speak blasphemies like this? Who can forgive sins but God alone?"
>
> But immediately, when Jesus perceived in His spirit that they reasoned thus within themselves, He said to them, "Why do you reason about these things in your hearts? Which is easier, to say to the paralytic, 'Your sins are forgiven you,' or to say, 'Arise, take up your bed and walk'? But that you may know that the Son of Man has power on earth to forgive sins"—He said to the paralytic, "I say to you, arise, take up your bed, and go to your house." Immediately he arose, took up the bed, and went out in the presence of them all, so that all were amazed and glorified God, saying, "We never saw anything like this!"

In the mind of our Lord Jesus, physical healing for our sickness, injury and pain is an indispensable element of forgiveness of sin (salvation). He did not view the two as separate works of grace but as one. What that means to us as believers is that as surely as we can confidently and fearlessly claim and experience the forgiveness of our sins through the blood of Jesus, we can with equal confidence and fearlessness claim and experience the divine healing of our bodies. We must not let doubt, fear, or uncertainty wedge its way into our hearts and minds concerning God's will for our healing. His Word clearly makes known His will.

Mark 1:40-41(NKJV)

Now a leper came to Him, imploring Him, kneeling down to Him and saying to Him, "If You are willing, You can make me clean."

Then Jesus, moved with compassion, stretched out His hand and touched him, and said to him, "I am willing; be cleansed."

"I am willing", says our compassionate Lord in the presence of a person suffering through disease. The will of God is for the sick to be healed now as just as Jesus healed them then.

Mark 8:16-17 (NKJV)

When evening had come, they brought to Him many who were demon-possessed. And He cast out the spirits with a word, and healed all who were sick, that it might be fulfilled which was spoken by Isaiah the prophet, saying: "He Himself took our infirmities And bore our sicknesses."

I Peter 2:24 (NKJV)

. . . who Himself bore our sins in His own body on the tree, that we, having died to sins, might live for righteousness—by whose stripes you were healed.

There is no disease, sickness, injury or condition of pain that the stripes of Jesus have not purchased healing for.

Psalm 103:2-3 (NKJV)

Bless the LORD, O my soul, and forget not all His benefits: Who forgives all your iniquities, Who heals all your diseases,

Jesus preached about healing and miracles in His first message in

Luke 4:17-19 (NKJV)

And He was handed the book of the prophet Isaiah. And when He had opened the book, He found the place where it was written: "The Spirit of the LORD is upon Me, because He has anointed Me to preach the gospel to the poor; He has sent Me to heal the brokenhearted, to proclaim liberty to the captives and recovery of sight

to the blind, to set at liberty those who are oppressed; to proclaim the acceptable
year of the LORD."

Three important elements were a consistent part of the ministry of Christ and must also
be incorporated into the practice of the church:
1. Teaching
2. Preaching the gospel of the Kingdom
3. Healing the sick

> Matthew 4:23 (NKJV)
> And Jesus went about all Galilee, teaching in their synagogues, preaching the gospel
> of the kingdom, and healing all kinds of sickness and all kinds of disease among the
> people.

These three elements represent the comprehensive ministry of Jesus Christ to mankind
then and now. He has not changed as the Bible declares in Heb 13:8 (NKJV):

Jesus Christ is the same yesterday and today and forever.

What He did then (save, heal, deliver) He still does now and will do forever.

One of the compound names of God in the Old Testament is found in
Exodus 15:26(NKJV):

> . . . and said, "If you diligently heed the voice of the LORD your God and do what
> is right in His sight, give ear to His commandments and keep all His statutes, I will
> put none of the diseases on you which I have brought on the Egyptians. For I am
> the LORD who heals you."

The phrase, "the Lord who heals you" is the Hebrew name "Yahweh-Rapha." Rapha
means: "to heal, cure, repair, mend, restore health." It comes from "rophe" which
means: "doctor, physician." No matter what illness or disease in body or mind you may
have, the Lord says to you, "I am your healer, your great physician, by My stripes you
have been healed."

The disciples were instructed by the Lord to bring healing to the hurting as they preached the gospel.

Matthew 10:1(NKJV)
And when He had called His twelve disciples to Him, He gave them power over unclean spirits, to cast them out, and to heal all kinds of sickness and all kinds of disease.

Matthew 10:7-8(NKJV)
And as you go, preach, saying, 'The kingdom of heaven is at hand.' Heal the sick, cleanse the lepers, raise the dead, cast out demons. Freely you have received, freely give.

Mark 16:15-20 (NKJV)
And He said to them, "Go into all the world and preach the gospel to every creature. He who believes and is baptized will be saved; but he who does not believe will be condemned. And these signs will follow those who believe: In My name they will cast out demons; they will speak with new tongues; they will take up serpents; and if they drink anything deadly, it will by no means hurt them; they will lay hands on the sick, and they will recover."

So then, after the Lord had spoken to them, He was received up into heaven, and sat down at the right hand of God. And they went out and preached everywhere, the Lord working with them and confirming the word through the accompanying signs. Amen.

Jesus said for His disciples (including you and me!) to lay our hands on the sick in the name of Jesus speaking healing to them. Jesus needs our hands and voice to touch and speak healing over broken and hurting bodies and lives. He heals them (confirming His word with signs following) when we obey His command to touch them in His name.

THE NAME OF JESUS AND DIVINE HEALING

The first recorded miracle of the early church is found in Acts 3:1-10 (NKJV):

> Now Peter and John went up together to the temple at the hour of prayer, the ninth
> hour. And a certain man lame from his mother's womb was carried, whom they
> laid daily at the gate of the temple which is called Beautiful, to ask alms from those
> who entered the temple; who, seeing Peter and John about to go into the temple,
> asked for alms. And fixing his eyes on him, with John, Peter said, "Look at us." So
> he gave them his attention, expecting to receive something from them.
>
> Then Peter said, "Silver and gold I do not have, but what I do have I give you:
> In the name of Jesus Christ of Nazareth, rise up and walk." And he took him by
> the right hand and lifted him up, and immediately his feet and ankle bones received
> strength. So he, leaping up, stood and walked and entered the temple with them—
> walking, leaping, and praising God. And all the people saw him walking and
> praising God. Then they knew that it was he who sat begging alms at the Beautiful
> Gate of the temple; and they were filled with wonder and amazement at what had
> happened to him.

In this narrative we see the basic elements needed in the work of divine healing. There
is a crippled man who had never walked. He is asking for alms at the gate of the temple.
Peter and John are approaching the gate and the crippled man asks for a gift.

Here are the three dynamic elements of a miracle:

Element #1: Expectation
The man looked up at Peter and John expecting to receive something from them. Expectation is the atmosphere where miracles flourish. If you're sick, expect to be healed
when you're prayed for. If you're praying over the sick, expect them to be healed. This is
what faith looks like; it expects to receive what God has promised.

Element #2: The Name of Jesus Christ
The second element in the successful outcome of the lame man's healing in Acts chapter
3 is the "Name of Jesus Christ." Peter said he didn't have any money with him but he
did have something more valuable and powerful than money, the name of Jesus Christ.

Every believer has the name of Jesus just like Peter had. There is no disease or sickness that is greater than the name of Jesus!

John 14:12-14 (NKJV)

"Most assuredly, I say to you, he who believes in Me, the works that I do he will do also; and greater works than these he will do, because I go to My Father. And whatever you ask in My name, that I will do, that the Father may be glorified in the Son. If you ask anything in My name, I will do it.

Peter made it clear how this man was healed in Acts 4:10 (NKJV):

. . . let it be known to you all, and to all the people of Israel, that by the name of Jesus Christ of Nazareth, whom you crucified, whom God raised from the dead, by Him this man stands here before you whole.

Acts 9:33-35 (NKJV)

There he found a certain man named Aeneas, who had been bedridden eight years and was paralyzed. And Peter said to him, "Aeneas, Jesus the Christ heals you. Arise and make your bed." Then he arose immediately. So all who dwelt at Lydda and Sharon saw him and turned to the Lord.

Philippians 2:9-11 (NKJV)

Therefore God also has highly exalted Him and given Him the name which is above every name, that at the name of Jesus every knee should bow, of those in heaven, and of those on earth, and of those under the earth, and that every tongue should confess that Jesus Christ is Lord, to the glory of God the Father.

When we speak healing to the sick in the name of Jesus Christ, it's as if Jesus himself were standing there healing the sick. Through His name we exercise His triumphant victory at the cross over sickness and disease and release His healing grace to a suffering world.

Element #3: Faith in the Name of Jesus

Peter gives a thorough explanation of how the lame man was healed in Acts 3:16 (NKJV):

> And His name, through faith in His name, has made this man strong, whom you see and know. Yes, the faith which comes through Him has given him this perfect soundness in the presence of you all.

Yes, His name healed him but it also took faith in His name to unlock the authority it holds to heal the sick and release miracles. To make sure that all the glory for this miracle was directed to God, Peter then declared that even the faith he used in prayer for the lame man came from God. God gave him the faith to believe in the power of the name of Jesus to accomplish the miracle. God will also give us the same quality of faith in the power residing in the glorious name of Jesus Christ.

Jesus said in Mark 16:17-18 (NKJV), "And these signs will follow those who believe: in my name . . . they will lay hands on the sick, and they will recover." When we believe in His name, His name heals all disease and sickness!

An important question is often asked about the subject of divine healing. Does God send sickness or disease into my life in order to teach me something?

Simple answer, no. Yes, God can speak to us and work good in our lives out of anything we experience, good or bad but we must be certain about the nature and origin of human suffering. It comes from sin and has been multiplied and intensified through the work of Satan. Jesus made this clear in John 10:10 (NKJV):

> The thief does not come except to steal, and to kill, and to destroy. I have come that they may have life, and that they may have it more abundantly.

The Bible declares this truth in James 1:16-17 (NKJV):

> Do not be deceived, my beloved brethren. Every good gift and every perfect gift

is from above, and comes down from the Father of lights, with whom there is no variation or shadow of turning.

Satan is the thief who uses sickness and suffering to steal, kill and destroy people's lives. Jesus is our Healer and Redeemer who has come to restore abundant life to all mankind. When the sick are healed it is a testimony of the resurrection of Jesus Christ from the grave. God loves to heal hurting lives and He's looking for any and every opportunity to heal people. If you're in need of healing, this is your day to receive God's gift and grace of healing. Just believe God's Word and receive God's gift of healing.

HERE ARE SEVERAL SCRIPTURAL METHODS FOR PRAYING FOR THOSE WHO NEED HEALING:

I. Laying on of hands.

> Mark 16:18(b)
> ". . . they will lay hands on the sick, and they will recover."

Laying on of hands is when a believer (or believers) physically touches someone while they're praying for their healing in Jesus name.

II. When the sick ask for prayer from church elders (recognized local church leaders), who then anoint them with oil while praying the prayer of faith.

> James 5:14-15 (NKJV)
> Is anyone among you sick? Let him call for the elders of the church, and let them pray over him, anointing him with oil in the name of the Lord. And the prayer of faith will save the sick, and the Lord will raise him up. And if he has committed sins, he will be forgiven.

> James 5:14-15 (MSG)
> Are you sick? Call the church leaders together to pray and anoint you with oil in the name of the Master. Believing-prayer will heal you, and Jesus will put you on your feet. And if you've sinned, you'll be forgiven—healed inside and out.

III. Prayer cloths. When an anointed believer prays over cloth that is then taken and laid on the sick.

Acts 19:11-12 (NKJV)

Now God worked unusual miracles by the hands of Paul, so that even handkerchiefs or aprons were brought from his body to the sick, and the diseases left them and the evil spirits went out of them.

Acts 19:11-12 (MSG)

God did powerful things through Paul, things quite out of the ordinary. The word got around and people started taking pieces of clothing—handkerchiefs and scarves and the like—that had touched Paul's skin and then touching the sick with them. The touch did it—they were healed and whole.

IV. Sending the word of healing to someone who's not physically present. Speaking healing in Jesus name to someone in need.

Psalm 107:20 (NKJV)

He sent His word and healed them, and delivered them from their destructions.

Matthew 8:8-13 (NKJV)

The centurion answered and said, "Lord, I am not worthy that You should come under my roof. But only speak a word, and my servant will be healed. For I also am a man under authority, having soldiers under me. And I say to this one, 'Go,' and he goes; and to another, 'Come,' and he comes; and to my servant, 'Do this,' and he does it."

When Jesus heard it, He marveled, and said to those who followed, "Assuredly, I say to you, I have not found such great faith, not even in Israel! And I say to you that many will come from east and west, and sit down with Abraham, Isaac, and Jacob in the kingdom of heaven. But the sons of the kingdom will be cast out into outer darkness. There will be weeping and gnashing of teeth." Then Jesus said to the centurion, "Go your way; and as you have believed, so let it be done for you." And his servant was healed that same hour.

V. Casting out a 'spirit of infirmity' (a demonic power that is afflicting someone with a disease).

Note, please, that Jesus did not 'cast out a demon' every time He healed the sick. When He discerned that a sickness had a demonic origin, He then dealt with the evil spirit. Conversely, He also healed multitudes without any mention of there being a demonic origin to their condition. We can summarize this balanced view that sometimes disease does have a demonic root and sometimes it does not. It is then imperative that we rely upon the unfailing leadership of the Holy Spirit when attempting to discern which expression of prayer is most appropriate for every situation.

CHAPTER 4
QUESTIONS AND ANSWERS

1. Jesus Christ is our Savior, Baptizer and _____.

2. Jesus bore the _____, _____, and _____ of all mankind at the cross!

3. Just as we as believers can confidently and fearlessly claim and experience forgiveness of our sins through the shed blood of Jesus, we can with equal _____ and _____claim the _____ _____ of our bodies!

4. What were the three important elements in the ministry of Christ?
   A. _____
   B. _____
   C. _____

5. Hebrews 13:8 tells us "Jesus Christ is the _____ yesterday, _____ and forever."

6. _____ is the atmosphere where miracles flourish!

7. When we speak healing to the sick in the _____ ____ _____ _____,
it's as if _____ Himself were standing there healing the sick!

8. In Mark 16:17(a) Jesus said, "These signs will follow those who _____
_____ _____, they will _____ _____ on the sick and they will
_____!"

9. _____ is the thief who used _____ and _____ to
steal, kill and destroy peoples' lives!

5 JESUS CHRIST OUR PROVIDER

Jesus Christ is our Savior, Baptizer, Healer and also our Heavenly Provider! Included in His all-encompassing plan of Redemption for mankind is the grace of divine provision for every need in our lives, including those that are earthly and material.

As we examine this wonderful blessing that our loving God has purchased for us through the blood of His Son, our foundation for faith and belief will be based on what the Bible has to say to us on this subject, not what some religious traditions or mens' opinions say. To approach this area of study (as well as any other) without basing the suppositions of our doctrine and faith on what is clearly and continually revealed in the scriptures, will allow mens' ideas and agendas to shape our beliefs rather than the eternal truths of God's inspired word.

By His very nature, our God is a provider. Before He created man as the crown jewel of all His glorious creation, He first thought of and provided all that man needed in the Garden of Eden. Jesus compared our Heavenly Father's caring heart for our needs to a human father who loves and cares for their children.

Matthew 7:7-11 (NKJV)

"Ask, and it will be given to you; seek, and you will find; knock, and it will be opened to you. For everyone who asks receives, and he who seeks finds, and to him who knocks it will be opened. Or what man is there among you who, if his son asks for bread, will give him a stone? Or if he asks for a fish, will he give him a serpent? If you then, being evil, know how to give good gifts to your children, how much more will your Father who is in heaven give good things to those who ask Him!

Matthew 7:7-11 (MSG)
"Don't bargain with God. Be direct. Ask for what you need. This isn't a cat-and-mouse, hide-and-seek game we're in. If your child asks for bread, do you trick him with sawdust? If he asks for fish, do you scare him with a live snake on his plate? As bad as you are, you wouldn't think of such a thing. You're at least decent to your own children. So don't you think the God who conceived you in love will be even better?

Jesus said the comparison between human fathers and our Heavenly Father is imperfect, because as human fathers we are imperfect and sinful men, so our love for our children, as strong and passionate as we may feel, cannot compare equally to our good, perfect, holy and eternally loving Heavenly Father's care and love for us. Of course, God cares about the real needs, circumstances, problems and desires of our lives, because we are His children.

THE GRACE OF OUR LORD JESUS CHRIST

God has a deep and eternal love for us. Motivated by that great love, He included in the redemptive work of Christ the grace of provision for our lives.

II Corinthians 8:9 (NKJV)
For you know the grace of our Lord Jesus Christ, that though He was rich, yet for your sakes He became poor, that you through His poverty might become rich.

Of course, this description of "you through His poverty might become rich" means much more than just being delivered from material poverty. It includes all the vast riches of His free grace for our lives: forgiveness of sins, the gift of His Holy Spirit, the healing of our lives, the receiving of His kingdom and so much more. But make no mistake about it, this verse of Scripture plainly and powerfully declares that this grace includes deliverance from the oppression and suffering of material poverty. Poverty is not a good thing; it is a very bad and evil thing. Only in the fanciful minds and imaginations of some in academic and religious circles in the western world has the concept of material poverty been given an elevated status of holding blessing and benefit to mankind. I have ministered in over five continents and dozens of countries around the world, and those who I ministered and witnessed to who lived in poverty were under great oppression and suffering. Poverty kills children. Poverty causes disease, death and destruction everywhere that it's present. There is no good side of this hideous condition. Poverty is the direct result of the fall of man and the curse of sin.

Genesis 3:17-19 (NKJV)
Then to Adam He said, "Because you have heeded the voice of your wife, and have eaten from the tree of which I commanded you, saying, 'You shall not eat of it': "Cursed is the ground for your sake; in toil you shall eat of it all the days of your life.
Both thorns and thistles it shall bring forth for you, and you shall eat the herb of the field.
    In the sweat of your face you shall eat bread till you return to the ground, for out of it you were taken; for dust you are, and to dust you shall return."

Christ Jesus died for us to deliver us from every consequence and penalty of sin, including poverty! The Bible declares His work in Galatians:

Galatians 3:13-14 (NLT)
But Christ has rescued us from the curse pronounced by the law. When he was hung on the cross, he took upon himself the curse for our wrongdoing. For it is written in the Scriptures, "Cursed is everyone who is hung on a tree." Through Christ Jesus, God has blessed the Gentiles with the same blessing he promised to Abraham, so that we who are believers might receive the promised Holy Spirit through faith.

The blood of Christ has redeemed our lives from the conviction, condemnation and curse of the law against us. (Remember, the purpose of the law was not to offer us another way of obtaining salvation through living sinlessly, perfect lives - that's impossible.

The entire function of the law is to convict all of us as guilty, in order to then qualify all of us for the gift of His free grace.)

Deuteronomy 28:15-20 (NLT)
"But if you refuse to listen to the Lord your God and do not obey all the commands and decrees I am giving you today, all these curses will come and overwhelm you:
Your towns and your fields will be cursed.
Your fruit baskets and breadboards will be cursed.
Your children and your crops will be cursed.
The offspring of your herds and flocks will be cursed.
Wherever you go and whatever you do, you will be cursed.
"The Lord himself will send on you curses, confusion, and frustration in everything you do, until at last you are completely destroyed for doing evil and abandoning me.

THE BLESSING OF ABRAHAM

God has now extended to be available to all mankind (gentiles, non-Jewish) the gift of the Jewish Messiah, Jesus Christ. The Messiah of the Jews is now also the Savior of all mankind. Salvation has been made available for everyone everywhere no matter what their race, religion or sex is. This is the mystery that the apostle Paul was entrusted to reveal to us in his writings in the New Testament, that God would engraft into the tree of His covenant people the Jews, the branch of believing gentiles. Now a vital component of the blessing of Abraham is material, financial provision and blessing.

Genesis 12:1-3 (NKJV)
Now the LORD had said to Abram: "Get out of your country, from your family and from your father's house, to a land that I will show you.
I will make you a great nation; I will bless you and make your name great; and you shall be a blessing.
    I will bless those who bless you, and I will curse him who curses you; and in you all the families of the earth shall be blessed."

God's promise to Abraham was two-fold:

1. "I will bless you"
2. "And you shall be a blessing"

In these two promises is the very intention, design and purpose of the blessing of God. God blesses us in order that we can then be a blessing to others. This is the definition of the purpose of prosperity in a person's life, to enable us to be a blessing and a resource to those in need. The blessed person becomes a blessing. God's promise becomes a reality in Abraham's life and family.

Genesis 13:2 (NKJV)
Abram was very rich in livestock, in silver, and in gold.

Genesis 24:35 (NKJV)
The LORD has blessed my master greatly, and he has become great; and He has given him flocks and herds, silver and gold, male and female servants, and camels and donkeys.

Genesis 26:12-13 (NKJV)
Then Isaac sowed in that land, and reaped in the same year a hundredfold; and the LORD blessed him. The man began to prosper, and continued prospering until he became very prosperous;

The grace of God's provision to our lives is also revealed in these powerful scriptures. Meditate on and memorize these great promises.

Phil 4:19 (NKJV)
And my God shall supply all your need according to His riches in glory by Christ Jesus.

Phil 4:19 (MSG)
You can be sure that God will take care of everything you need, his generosity exceeding even yours in the glory that pours from Jesus.

Phil 4:19 (AMP)

And my God will liberally supply (fill to the full) your every need according to His riches in glory in Christ Jesus.

Ps 23:1 (NKJV)
The LORD is my shepherd; I shall not want.

Ps 23:1 (NLT)
The Lord is my shepherd; I have all that I need.

Ps 23:1 (AMP)
THE LORD is my Shepherd [to feed, guide, and shield me], I shall not lack.

Ps 34:9-10 (NKJV)
Oh, fear the LORD, you His saints! There is no want to those who fear Him. The young lions lack and suffer hunger; but those who seek the LORD shall not lack any good thing.

Ps 34:9-10 (NLT)
Fear the Lord, you his godly people, for those who fear him will have all they need. Even strong young lions sometimes go hungry, but those who trust in the Lord will lack no good thing.

Ps 34:9-10 (AMP)
O fear the Lord, you His saints [revere and worship Him]! For there is no want to those who truly revere and worship Him with godly fear. The young lions lack food and suffer hunger, but they who seek (inquire of and require) the Lord [by right of their need and on the authority of His Word], none of them shall lack any beneficial thing.

Ps 37:25 (NKJV)
I have been young, and now am old; yet I have not seen the righteous forsaken, nor his descendants begging bread.

Prosperity for the believer is simply this, having enough provision to fulfill our divine purpose. Our divine purpose is that predestined design that God created our lives to fulfill. Our life's purpose can only be found through knowing and following Jesus Christ.

Acts 9:1-6 (NKJV)

Then Saul, still breathing threats and murder against the disciples of the Lord, went to the high priest and asked letters from him to the synagogues of Damascus, so that if he found any who were of the Way, whether men or women, he might bring them bound to Jerusalem.

As he journeyed he came near Damascus, and suddenly a light shone around him from heaven. Then he fell to the ground, and heard a voice saying to him, "Saul, Saul, why are you persecuting Me?"

And he said, "Who are You, Lord?" Then the Lord said, "I am Jesus, whom you are persecuting. It is hard for you to kick against the goads."

So he, trembling and astonished, said, "Lord, what do You want me to do?" Then the Lord said to him, "Arise and go into the city, and you will be told what you must do."

The two great questions of life were asked by Saul that day:
1. Who are You, Lord?
2. What do you want me to do?

The 'what' or purpose of our lives can only be found by knowing the 'who' of all of life which is the person of Jesus Christ. When we discover the 'who', He reveals the 'what'. When we follow the person of Christ, He reveals the purpose of God for our lives. When we find the purpose of life by walking with the person of Jesus, we qualify for access into the realm of heavenly abundance that makes our divine purpose a reality. When our hearts are fully engaged in the pursuit of God's will, that is when His supply of grace is most readily available for all our lives. Jesus taught about this in Matthew 6.

Matthew 6:24-34 (NKJV)

"No one can serve two masters; for either he will hate the one and love the other, or else he will be loyal to the one and despise the other. You cannot serve God and mammon.

"Therefore I say to you, do not worry about your life, what you will eat or what you will drink; nor about your body, what you will put on. Is not life more than food and the body more than clothing? Look at the birds of the air, for they neither sow nor reap nor gather into barns; yet your heavenly Father feeds them. Are you not of more value than they? Which of you by worrying can add one cubit to his stature?

"So why do you worry about clothing? Consider the lilies of the field, how they grow: they neither toil nor spin; and yet I say to you that even Solomon in all his glory was not arrayed like one of these. Now if God so clothes the grass of the field, which today is, and tomorrow is thrown into the oven, will He not much more clothe you, O you of little faith?

"Therefore do not worry, saying, 'What shall we eat?' or 'What shall we drink?' or 'What shall we wear?' For after all these things the Gentiles seek. For your heavenly Father knows that you need all these things. But seek first the kingdom of God and His righteousness, and all these things shall be added to you. Therefore do not worry about tomorrow, for tomorrow will worry about its own things. Sufficient for the day is its own trouble.

Matthew 6:24-34 (MSG)
"You can't worship two gods at once. Loving one god, you'll end up hating the other. Adoration of one feeds contempt for the other. You can't worship God and Money both.

"If you decide for God, living a life of God-worship, it follows that you don't fuss about what's on the table at mealtimes or whether the clothes in your closet are in fashion. There is far more to your life than the food you put in your stomach, more to your outer appearance than the clothes you hang on your body. Look at the birds, free and unfettered, not tied down to a job description, careless in the care of God. And you count far more to him than birds.

"Has anyone by fussing in front of the mirror ever gotten taller by so much as an inch? All this time and money wasted on fashion—do you think it makes that much difference? Instead of looking at the fashions, walk out into the fields and look at the wildflowers. They never primp or shop, but have you ever seen color and design quite like it? The ten best-dressed men and women in the country look shabby alongside them.

"If God gives such attention to the appearance of wildflowers—most of which are never even seen—don't you think he'll attend to you, take pride in you, do his best for you? What I'm trying to do here is to get you to relax, to not be so preoccupied with getting, so you can respond to God's giving. People who don't know God and the way he works fuss over these things, but you know both God and how he works. Steep your life in God-reality, God-initiative, God-provisions. Don't worry about missing out. You'll find all your everyday human concerns will be met.

"Give your entire attention to what God is doing right now, and don't get worked up about what may or may not happen tomorrow. God will help you deal with whatever hard things come up when the time comes.

Jesus gave us a beautiful summation of this powerful truth in verse 33: "but seek first the kingdom of God and His righteousness, and all these things will be added unto you." As we put God first place in our life, He will add all we need to our lives. When our hearts and minds are in right priority, God's provision and prosperity will flow to us supernaturally. We're not called to be 'blessing seekers' or 'money seekers,' we're called to be 'God seekers.' When we truly live with a right priority to pursue God's kingdom and will, we qualify for the promise of divine provision meeting all our lives needs.
We see then that prosperity for believers is an external manifestation of the internal transformation of our hearts and minds as this next scripture declares.

3 John 1:2 (NKJV)
Beloved, I pray that you may prosper in all things and be in health, just as your soul prospers.

This is the prayer of the Apostle John for his beloved friend, Gaius. It reveals the longing of God's heart for us to experience health and prosperity in our life as His beloved children. The secret to both of these blessings is revealed in the last sentence, "even as your soul prospers." For the life of His children, both physical health and financial prosperity are the direct result of a healthy, prosperous soul. When our internal world is healthy, then our external world will exhibit the same qualities of blessings.

Proverbs 23:7(a) (NKJV)

For as he thinks in his heart, so is he.

When we allow a spiritual renovation to occur in our heart and mind, renewal then is reflected in the rest of our lives.

Romans 12:2 (NKJV)
And do not be conformed to this world, but be transformed by the renewing of your mind, that you may prove what is that good and acceptable and perfect will of God.

When we purposely flood our thought life with the light of God's Word, we then will begin to experience God's Word working in us through all our life.

Psalm 1:1-3 (NKJV)
Blessed is the man who walks not in the counsel of the ungodly, nor stands in the path of sinners, nor sits in the seat of the scornful; But his delight is in the law of the LORD, and in His law he meditates day and night. He shall be like a tree planted by the rivers of water, that brings forth its fruit in its season, whose leaf also shall not wither; and whatever he does shall prosper.

Psalm 1:1-3 (MSG)
How well God must like you— you don't hang out at Sin Saloon, you don't slink along Dead-End Road, you don't go to Smart-Mouth College.
    Instead you thrill to God's Word, you chew on Scripture day and night. You're a tree replanted in Eden, bearing fresh fruit every month, never dropping a leaf, always in blossom.

Psalm 1:1-3 (AMP)
BLESSED (HAPPY, fortunate, prosperous, and enviable) is the man who walks and lives not in the counsel of the ungodly [following their advice, their plans and purposes], nor stands [submissive and inactive] in the path where sinners walk, nor sits down [to relax and rest] where the scornful [and the mockers] gather.
    But his delight and desire are in the law of the Lord, and on His law (the precepts, the instructions, the teachings of God) he habitually meditates (ponders and

studies) by day and by night.

And he shall be like a tree firmly planted [and tended] by the streams of water, ready to bring forth its fruit in its season; its leaf also shall not fade or wither; and everything he does shall prosper [and come to maturity].

John 1:7-8 (NKJV)
This man came for a witness, to bear witness of the Light, that all through him might believe. He was not that Light, but was sent to bear witness of that Light.

John 1:7-8 (AMP)
This man came to witness, that he might testify of the Light, that all men might believe in it [adhere to it, trust it, and rely upon it] through him.

He was not the Light himself, but came that he might bear witness regarding the Light.

God promises success and prosperity to us if we put His word first place in our lives by meditating on it day and night. We do that when we introduce and then retain the promises of God's Word into our conscience thought life. His word will transform us from the inside out and produce the fruit of prosperity and success.

In the first part of this chapter we exposed you to the wonderful promise of God's provision to meet your needs. Now, we'll look into the scripture principles that allow us to experience the power of God's promise.

DIVINE ECONOMICS

To fully experience the quality of grace that the scriptures promise us, we first fully engage in the scripture principles that are revealed as an irreplaceable element of that promise in Scripture. The promise of receiving is always preceded by the practice of giving first.

Jesus said in Luke 6:38 (NKJV):

Give, and it will be given to you: good measure, pressed down, shaken together, and running over will be put into your bosom. For with the same measure that you use, it will be measured back to you."

Luke 6:38 (MSG)

Give away your life; you'll find life given back, but not merely given back—given back with bonus and blessing. Giving, not getting, is the way. Generosity begets generosity."

Luke 6:38 (NLT)

Give, and you will receive. Your gift will return to you in full—pressed down, shaken together to make room for more, running over, and poured into your lap. The amount you give will determine the amount you get back.

This principle is identified as "the law of sowing and reaping." Like the natural and universal law of gravity on the earth, the spiritual law of sowing and reaping (giving and receiving) governs all of our behavior and experience in the kingdom of God. In the mindset of the unsaved world they covet, grasp and they hold securely what they desired and obtained. In the life of God's people we are called to live much differently than the selfishness that the world is controlled by. We are called to be 'givers' not just 'takers.' We can joyfully experience the satisfaction that only givers receive, because we know that when we give something we are actually planting a seed that will eventually return to us in a harvest of blessing and favor from God. This powerful principle is taught in these scriptures:

II Corinthians 9:6-10 (NKJV)

But this I say: He who sows sparingly will also reap sparingly, and he who sows bountifully will also reap bountifully. So let each one give as he purposes in his heart, not grudgingly or of necessity; for God loves a cheerful giver. And God is able to make all grace abound toward you, that you, always having all sufficiency in all things, may have an abundance for every good work. As it is written: "He has dispersed abroad, He has given to the poor; His righteousness endures forever."

Now may He who supplies seed to the sower, and bread for food, supply and multiply the seed you have sown and increase the fruits of your righteousness,

II Corinthians 9:6-10 (MSG)

Remember: A stingy planter gets a stingy crop; a lavish planter gets a lavish crop. I want each of you to take plenty of time to think it over, and make up your own mind what you will give. That will protect you against sob stories and arm-twisting. God loves it when the giver delights in the giving.

God can pour on the blessings in astonishing ways so that you're ready for anything and everything, more than just ready to do what needs to be done. As one psalmist puts it, He throws caution to the winds, giving to the needy in reckless abandon. His right-living, right-giving ways never run out, never wear out. This most generous God who gives seed to the farmer that becomes bread for your meals is more than extravagant with you.

II Corinthians 9:6-10 (AMP)

[Remember] this: he who sows sparingly and grudgingly will also reap sparingly and grudgingly, and he who sows generously [that blessings may come to someone] will also reap generously and with blessings.

Let each one [give] as he has made up his own mind and purposed in his heart, not reluctantly or sorrowfully or under compulsion, for God loves (He takes pleasure in, prizes above other things, and is unwilling to abandon or to do without) a cheerful (joyous, "prompt to do it") giver [whose heart is in his giving].

And God is able to make all grace (every favor and earthly blessing) come to you in abundance, so that you may always and under all circumstances and whatever the need be self-sufficient [possessing enough to require no aid or support and furnished in abundance for every good work and charitable donation].

As it is written, He [the benevolent person] scatters abroad; He gives to the poor; His deeds of justice and goodness and kindness and benevolence will go on and endure forever!

And [God] Who provides seed for the sower and bread for eating will also provide and multiply your [resources for] sowing and increase the fruits of your righteousness [which manifests itself in active goodness, kindness, and charity].

Proverbs 11:24-25 (NKJV)

There is one who scatters, yet increases more; and there is one who withholds more than is right, but it leads to poverty.

The generous soul will be made rich, and he who waters will also be watered himself.

Proverbs 11:24-25 (MSG)
The world of the generous gets larger and larger; the world of the stingy gets smaller and smaller.

The one who blesses others is abundantly blessed; those who help others are helped.

Proverbs 11:24-25 (AMP)
There are those who [generously] scatter abroad, and yet increase more; there are those who withhold more than is fitting or what is justly due, but it results only in want.

The liberal person shall be enriched, and he who waters shall himself be watered.

Galatians 6:6-10 (NKJV)
Let him who is taught the word share in all good things with him who teaches. Do not be deceived, God is not mocked; for whatever a man sows, that he will also reap. For he who sows to his flesh will of the flesh reap corruption, but he who sows to the Spirit will of the Spirit reap everlasting life. And let us not grow weary while doing good, for in due season we shall reap if we do not lose heart. Therefore, as we have opportunity, let us do good to all, especially to those who are of the household of faith.

Galatians 6:6-10 (MSG)
Be very sure now, you who have been trained to a self-sufficient maturity, that you enter into a generous common life with those who have trained you, sharing all the good things that you have and experience.

Don't be misled: No one makes a fool of God. What a person plants, he will harvest. The person who plants selfishness, ignoring the needs of others—ignoring God!—harvests a crop of weeds. All he'll have to show for his life is weeds! But the one who plants in response to God, letting God's Spirit do the growth work in him, harvests a crop of real life, eternal life.

So let's not allow ourselves to get fatigued doing good. At the right time we will harvest a good crop if we don't give up, or quit. Right now, therefore, every time we get the chance, let us work for the benefit of all, starting with the people closest to us in the community of faith.

Galatians 6:6-10 (AMP)

Let him who receives instruction in the Word [of God] share all good things with his teacher [contributing to his support].

Do not be deceived and deluded and misled; God will not allow Himself to be sneered at (scorned, disdained, or mocked by mere pretensions or professions, or by His precepts being set aside.) [He inevitably deludes himself who attempts to delude God.] For whatever a man sows, that and that only is what he will reap.

For he who sows to his own flesh (lower nature, sensuality) will from the flesh reap decay and ruin and destruction, but he who sows to the Spirit will from the Spirit reap eternal life.

And let us not lose heart and grow weary and faint in acting nobly and doing right, for in due time and at the appointed season we shall reap, if we do not loosen and relax our courage and faint.

So then, as occasion and opportunity open up to us, let us do good [morally] to all people [not only being useful or profitable to them, but also doing what is for their spiritual good and advantage]. Be mindful to be a blessing, especially to those of the household of faith [those who belong to God's family with you, the believers].

WHAT DO THE SCRIPTURES TEACH ABOUT GIVING?

The Bible teaches us that we are to give a tenth of our income to God. This is called the 'tithe' and we give it to God through being a part of and giving our 'tithe' to the local church we attend. Abraham gave a tithe to God in Genesis 14:18-20 (NKJV):

Then Melchizedek king of Salem brought out bread and wine; he was the priest of God Most High. And he blessed him and said: "Blessed be Abram of God Most High, Possessor of heaven and earth; and blessed be God Most High, Who has delivered your enemies into your hand." And he gave him a tithe of all.

It is through the giving of our tithe (10% of our income or wealth) that we qualify for God's economy.

Malachi 3:8-12 (NKJV)

"Will a man rob God? Yet you have robbed Me! But you say, 'In what way have we robbed You?' In tithes and offerings.

You are cursed with a curse, for you have robbed Me, even this whole nation.

Bring all the tithes into the storehouse, that there may be food in My house, and try Me now in this," says the LORD of hosts,

"If I will not open for you the windows of heaven and pour out for you such blessing that there will not be room enough to receive it.

"And I will rebuke the devourer for your sakes, so that he will not destroy the fruit of your ground, nor shall the vine fail to bear fruit for you in the field," says the LORD of hosts; And all nations will call you blessed, for you will be a delightful land," says the LORD of hosts.

Malachi 3:8-12 (NLT)

"Should people cheat God? Yet you have cheated me! "But you ask, 'What do you mean? When did we ever cheat you?'

"You have cheated me of the tithes and offerings due to me. You are under a curse, for your whole nation has been cheating me. Bring all the tithes into the storehouse so there will be enough food in my Temple. If you do," says the Lord of Heaven's Armies, "I will open the windows of heaven for you. I will pour out a blessing so great you won't have enough room to take it in! Try it! Put me to the test! Your crops will be abundant, for I will guard them from insects and disease. Your grapes will not fall from the vine before they are ripe," says the Lord of Heaven's Armies. "Then all nations will call you blessed, for your land will be such a delight," says the Lord of Heaven's Armies.

Look at the seven blessings God gives to those who tithe:

1. God will open the windows of heaven over their lives (receiving).
2. He will pour out such a great blessing you won't have room enough to contain it (abundance).
3. He will rebuke the devourer, Satan (delivering).
4. Our fruit will not be destroyed (protection).

5. Success in our life (blessing on children, business).

6. All nations (people) will call you blessed (great testimony to others).

7. You shall be a delight (joy, satisfaction, fulfillment, favor).

The blessing of Abraham for material provision and prosperity is initiated in our lives when we engage in the lifestyle of being a tither and giver. God introduces a challenge to us; He invites us to "prove Him," "try Him," "test Him" through our tithe. He dares us to give Him the opportunity to lavish our lives with His providing grace by becoming tithers. When we refuse to give Him our tithe we literally 'rob' Him of the opportunity to show us how gloriously He can meet our every need.

Luke 12:10-13 (NKJV)

"And anyone who speaks a word against the Son of Man, it will be forgiven him; but to him who blasphemes against the Holy Spirit, it will not be forgiven.

"Now when they bring you to the synagogues and magistrates and authorities, do not worry about how or what you should answer, or what you should say. For the Holy Spirit will teach you in that very hour what you ought to say."

Luke 12:10-13 (MSG)

"If you bad-mouth the Son of Man out of misunderstanding or ignorance, that can be overlooked. But if you're knowingly attacking God himself, taking aim at the Holy Spirit, that won't be overlooked.

"When they drag you into their meeting places, or into police courts and before judges, don't worry about defending yourselves—what you'll say or how you'll say it. The right words will be there. The Holy Spirit will give you the right words when the time comes."

Our lives are tested by how we think and behave about money. If we fail the test of being faithful with money to God, we also are then disqualified from other greater kingdom purposes and promotions. Our true heart is revealed by our relationship with money.

Matthew 6:21 (New King James Version)

For where your treasure is, there your heart will be also.

Matthew 6:21 (The Message)
The place where your treasure is, is the place you will most want to be, and end up being.

ALMS - GIFTS TO THE POOR

Another very important element in our lives as followers of Christ is the place of giving money and resources to those who are in need. Throughout Scripture there is both the command to care for the poor and as a consequence the promised blessing from God for choosing to do so.

Psalm 41:1-3 (NKJV)
Blessed is he who considers the poor; the LORD will deliver him in time of trouble.
The LORD will preserve him and keep him alive, and he will be blessed on the earth; You will not deliver him to the will of his enemies.
The LORD will strengthen him on his bed of illness; You will sustain him on his sickbed.

Psalm 41:1-3 (NLT)
Oh, the joys of those who are kind to the poor! The Lord rescues them when they are in trouble.
The Lord protects them and keeps them alive. He gives them prosperity in the land and rescues them from their enemies.
The Lord nurses them when they are sick and restores them to health.

Look at the many rewards God gives to those who give to the poor:
1. The Lord will deliver them.
2. The Lord will protect them.
3. The Lord will bless and prosper them.
4. The Lord will rescue them.
5. The Lord will strengthen and keep them.

Proverbs 19:17 (NLT)

If you help the poor, you are lending to the Lord—and he will repay you!

Proverbs 19:17 (MSG)
Mercy to the needy is a loan to God, and God pays back those loans in full.

Proverbs 19:17 (NKJV)
He who has pity on the poor lends to the LORD, and He will pay back what he has given.

We are literally 'lending to God' when we give to the poor. It is a loan that He will always happily repay us for giving (with interest!)

In Acts 10:1-4 (NKJV) we read:

There was a certain man in Caesarea called Cornelius, a centurion of what was called the Italian Regiment, a devout man and one who feared God with all his household, who gave alms generously to the people, and prayed to God always. About the ninth hour of the day he saw clearly in a vision an angel of God coming in and saying to him, "Cornelius!"
And when he observed him, he was afraid, and said, "What is it, lord?"
So he said to him, "Your prayers and your alms have come up for a memorial before God."

Cornelius was a man who did two things so powerfully that they built a memorial to God in Heaven. He prayed to God always and secondly, he gave alms (gifts to the poor) generously. Take note that his almsgiving literally arrested the attention of Almighty God who then sent an angel to begin a season of remarkable miracles in His life. Here are some simple elements of truth for us to live by:

- You cannot outgive God.
- You cannot give and not receive.
- We cannot reap where we have not sown.
- We determine the size of our harvest by the size of our seed.
- We conquer greed by becoming givers.

- Our treasure (what's most important to us) is revealed where we spend our time and money.
- You cannot be a blessing without first being blessed.

CHAPTER 5
QUESTIONS AND ANSWERS

1. By His very _____ our God is a _____.

2. The Bible says in II Cor. 8:9 "For you know the _____ of our Lord Jesus Christ, that though he was _____ yet for your sake He became _____ that you through His poverty might be made _____."

3. This verse plainly declares that the grace of our Lord Jesus Christ includes _____ from the _____ and _____ of _____ _____.

4. Poverty is a direct result of the _____ ___ _____ and the _____ ___ _____.

5. What is the two-fold promise of God to Abraham?
    1.
    2.

6. Phil 4:19 reads, "My God shall _____ __ __ _____ according to His _____ __ _____ by _____ _____."

7. Prosperity for the believer is simply this _____ _____ _____ __ _____ __ _____ _____.

8. Jesus said if we would _____ _____ _____ _____ _____ ___ _____ then all these things would be _____ _____ _____.

9. For the life of the Christian both _____ _____ and _____ _____ are the direct result of a _____ _____ soul.

10. The _____ ___ _____ ____ _____ is like the natural law of gravity on earth.

11. What 7 things happen in the life of a person?

_____

_____

_____

_____

_____

_____

_____

12. What are the 5 things God does for those who give to the poor? (Ps 41:1-3)

_____

_____

_____

_____

_____

13. You cannot _____ _____ God.

6 JESUS CHRIST OUR KING

Our Lord Jesus is coming back soon! The Bible teaches us that in the last days Jesus will once again come to the earth to claim His people, judge the nations, bring the heavenly Jerusalem, reign for one thousand years, cast Satan into eternal damnation, and create a new Heaven and earth. The Second Coming of Lord Jesus is told in Acts 1:9-11 and Daniel 7:13-14.

Acts 1:9-11 (NKJV)

Now when He had spoken these things, while they watched, He was taken up, and a cloud received Him out of their sight. And while they looked steadfastly toward heaven as He went up, behold, two men stood by them in white apparel, who also said, "Men of Galilee, why do you stand gazing up into heaven? This same Jesus, who was taken up from you into heaven, will so come in like manner as you saw Him go into heaven."

Daniel 7:13-14 (NKJV)

"I was watching in the night visions, and behold, One like the Son of Man, coming with the clouds of heaven! He came to the Ancient of Days, and they brought Him near before Him.

Then to Him was given dominion and glory and a kingdom, that all peoples, nations, and languages should serve Him. His dominion is an everlasting dominion, which shall not pass away, and His kingdom the one which shall not be destroyed.

When Christ comes back, the Bible describes what will transpire in that moment in I Thess. 4:13-18 (NKJV):

But I do not want you to be ignorant, brethren, concerning those who have fallen asleep, lest you sorrow as others who have no hope. For if we believe that Jesus died and rose again, even so God will bring with Him those who sleep in Jesus.

For this we say to you by the word of the Lord, that we who are alive and remain until the coming of the Lord will by no means precede those who are asleep. For the Lord Himself will descend from heaven with a shout, with the voice of an archangel, and with the trumpet of God. And the dead in Christ will rise first. Then we who are alive and remain shall be caught up together with them in the clouds to meet the Lord in the air. And thus we shall always be with the Lord. Therefore comfort one another with these words.

Here are five truths from this passage:
1. The Lord Himself will descend with a shout!
2. The voice of an archangel shall be heard.
3. The trumpet of God will sound.
4. The dead believers shall be raised to life.
5. Believers who are alive will be raptured ('caught up') in the clouds to meet the Lord.

The teaching of the 'rapture' (the catching up of believers) comes from the Latin translation of the Bible from this passage (simul rapiemur cum illis). Upon these clear points of the Christian church is near universal agreement. The scriptures, though, have purposely hidden the timelines and exact sequence of the prophetically declared other events up to the Rapture and Second Coming. We are told simply to live as if they could come at our next breath.

OUR BLESSED HOPE

The Bible says that all believers are to live with the "blessed hope" of our Lord's appearing.

Titus 2:11-14 (NKJV)

For the grace of God that brings salvation has appeared to all men, teaching us that, denying ungodliness and worldly lusts, we should live soberly, righteously, and godly in the present age, looking for the blessed hope and glorious appearing of our great God and Savior Jesus Christ, who gave Himself for us, that He might redeem us from every lawless deed and purify for Himself His own special people, zealous for good works.

Titus 2:11-14 (MSG)

God's readiness to give and forgive is now public. Salvation's available for everyone! We're being shown how to turn our backs on a godless, indulgent life, and how to take on a God-filled, God-honoring life. This new life is starting right now, and is whetting our appetites for the glorious day when our great God and Savior, Jesus Christ, appears. He offered himself as a sacrifice to free us from a dark, rebellious life into this good, pure life, making us a people he can be proud of, energetic in goodness.

The Bible warns us against being seduced by skeptics, scoffers and false teaching that denies or belittles the promise of the second coming of Christ.

II Peter 3:1-14 (NKJV)

Beloved, I now write to you this second epistle (in both of which I stir up your pure minds by way of reminder), that you may be mindful of the words which were spoken before by the holy prophets, and of the commandment of us, the apostles of the Lord and Savior, knowing this first: that scoffers will come in the last days, walking according to their own lusts, and saying, "Where is the promise of His coming? For since the fathers fell asleep, all things continue as they were from the beginning of creation." For this they willfully forget: that by the word of God the heavens were of old, and the earth standing out of water and in the water, by which the world that then existed perished, being flooded with water. But the heavens and the earth which are now preserved by the same word, are reserved for fire until the day of judgment and perdition of ungodly men.

But, beloved, do not forget this one thing, that with the Lord one day is as a thousand years, and a thousand years as one day. The Lord is not slack concerning His promise, as some count slackness, but is longsuffering toward us, not willing that any should perish but that all should come to repentance.

But the day of the Lord will come as a thief in the night, in which the heavens will pass away with a great noise, and the elements will melt with fervent heat; both the earth and the works that are in it will be burned up. Therefore, since all these things will be dissolved, what manner of persons ought you to be in holy conduct and godliness, looking for and hastening the coming of the day of God, because of which the heavens will be dissolved, being on fire, and the elements will melt with fervent heat? Nevertheless we, according to His promise, look for new heavens and a new earth in which righteousness dwells.

Therefore, beloved, looking forward to these things, be diligent to be found by Him in peace, without spot and blameless;

II Peter 3:1-14 (MSG)

My dear friends, this is now the second time I've written to you, both letters reminders to hold your minds in a state of undistracted attention. Keep in mind what the holy prophets said, and the command of our Master and Savior that was passed on by your apostles.

First off, you need to know that in the last days, mockers are going to have a heyday. Reducing everything to the level of their puny feelings, they'll mock, "So what's happened to the promise of his Coming? Our ancestors are dead and buried, and everything's going on just as it has from the first day of creation. Nothing's changed."

They conveniently forget that long ago all the galaxies and this very planet were brought into existence out of watery chaos by God's word. Then God's word brought the chaos back in a flood that destroyed the world. The current galaxies and earth are fuel for the final fire. God is poised, ready to speak his word again, ready to give the signal for the judgment and destruction of the desecrating skeptics.

Don't overlook the obvious here, friends. With God, one day is as good as a thousand years, a thousand years as a day. God isn't late with his promise as some measure lateness. He is restraining himself on account of you, holding back the End because he doesn't want anyone lost. He's giving everyone space and time to change.

But when the Day of God's Judgment does come, it will be unannounced, like a thief. The sky will collapse with a thunderous bang, everything disintegrating in a huge conflagration, earth and all its works exposed to the scrutiny of Judgment.

Since everything here today might well be gone tomorrow, do you see how essential it is to live a holy life? Daily expect the Day of God, eager for its arrival. The galaxies will burn up and the elements melt down that day—but we'll hardly notice. We'll be looking the other way, ready for the promised new heavens and the promised new earth, all landscaped with righteousness.

So, my dear friends, since this is what you have to look forward to, do your very best to be found living at your best, in purity and peace.

Here are some of the main points from these verses concerning the second coming of Christ:

1. The second coming of Christ will be scoffed at by many in the last days.
2. We are reminded that God does not exist in or have the same limitations and control from time that we do, a day is like a thousand years with the Lord.
3. We are given beautiful insight into what motivates any delay in God's decision to send His Son - "not willing that any should perish but that all should come to repentance." God's heart so longs for more people to be saved that He's willing to adjust, and even delay the coming of His Son for one more man's soul to be saved!
4. The day of the Lord (the day of the second coming of Christ) will come as a thief in the night.
5. All the universe, including the earth, shall be destroyed and then recreated.
6. We are to live with the constant awareness and personal accountability that such knowledge should produce in our hearts, "what manner of persons ought ye to be in holy conduct and godliness."
7. By fervently looking for His soon coming, we then become more quickly engaged in obedience to His work and Spirit to spread the gospel to others and allow our lives to be prepared as His bride, thus we 'hasten' or speed up the day of His coming.

Our Lord also taught at some length about the time of His second coming.

Matthew 24:3-44 (NKJV)

Then Jesus went out and departed from the temple, and His disciples came up to show Him the buildings of the temple. And Jesus said to them, "Do you not see all these things? Assuredly, I say to you, not one stone shall be left here upon another, that shall not be thrown down."

Now as He sat on the Mount of Olives, the disciples came to Him privately, saying, "Tell us, when will these things be? And what will be the sign of Your coming, and of the end of the age?"

And Jesus answered and said to them: "Take heed that no one deceives you. For many will come in My name, saying, 'I am the Christ,' and will deceive many. And you will hear of wars and rumors of wars. See that you are not troubled; for all these things must come to pass, but the end is not yet. For nation will rise against nation, and kingdom against kingdom. And there will be famines, pestilences, and earthquakes in various places. All these are the beginning of sorrows.

"Then they will deliver you up to tribulation and kill you, and you will be hated by all nations for My name's sake. And then many will be offended, will betray one another, and will hate one another. Then many false prophets will rise up and deceive many. And because lawlessness will abound, the love of many will grow cold. But he who endures to the end shall be saved. And this gospel of the kingdom will be preached in all the world as a witness to all the nations, and then the end will come.

"Therefore when you see the 'abomination of desolation,' spoken of by Daniel the prophet, standing in the holy place" (whoever reads, let him understand), "then let those who are in Judea flee to the mountains. Let him who is on the housetop not go down to take anything out of his house.

And let him who is in the field not go back to get his clothes. But woe to those who are pregnant and to those who are nursing babies in those days! And pray that your flight may not be in winter or on the Sabbath. For then there will be great tribulation, such as has not been since the beginning of the world until this time, no, nor ever shall be. And unless those days were shortened, no flesh would be saved; but for the elect's sake those days will be shortened.

"Then if anyone says to you, 'Look, here is the Christ!' or 'There!' do not believe it. For false christs and false prophets will rise and show great signs and wonders to deceive, if possible, even the elect. See, I have told you beforehand.

"Therefore if they say to you, 'Look, He is in the desert!' do not go out; or 'Look,

He is in the inner rooms!' do not believe it. For as the lightning comes from the east and flashes to the west, so also will the coming of the Son of Man be. For wherever the carcass is, there the eagles will be gathered together.

"Immediately after the tribulation of those days the sun will be darkened, and the moon will not give its light; the stars will fall from heaven, and the powers of the heavens will be shaken. Then the sign of the Son of Man will appear in heaven, and then all the tribes of the earth will mourn, and they will see the Son of Man coming on the clouds of heaven with power and great glory. And He will send His angels with a great sound of a trumpet, and they will gather together His elect from the four winds, from one end of heaven to the other.

"Now learn this parable from the fig tree: When its branch has already become tender and puts forth leaves, you know that summer is near. So you also, when you see all these things, know that it is near—at the doors! Assuredly, I say to you, this generation will by no means pass away till all these things take place. Heaven and earth will pass away, but My words will by no means pass away.

"But of that day and hour no one knows, not even the angels of heaven, but My Father only. But as the days of Noah were, so also will the coming of the Son of Man be. For as in the days before the flood, they were eating and drinking, marrying and giving in marriage, until the day that Noah entered the ark, and did not know until the flood came and took them all away, so also will the coming of the Son of Man be. Then two men will be in the field: one will be taken and the other left. Two women will be grinding at the mill: one will be taken and the other left. Watch therefore, for you do not know what hour your Lord is coming. But know this, that if the master of the house had known what hour the thief would come, he would have watched and not allowed his house to be broken into. Therefore you also be ready, for the Son of Man is coming at an hour you do not expect."

Jesus said the last days, the time just before and leading up to His coming, will be a time of:

1. Great deception (most repeated sign of the last days)
2. Wars and rumors of wars
3. Ethnic unrest (nation- 'ethnos') racial tension
4. Nations warring against other nations
5. Kingdoms in conflict and war

6. Famines (1 billion people went without food today)

7. Pestilences (AIDS, bird flu, swine flu, etc.)

8. Earthquakes in unusual places

9. Tribulation (pressure, stress, persecution)

10. Offense (easily offended people)

11. Betrayal (broken relationships)

12. Many false prophets

13. Lawlessness (it will abound)

14. The love of many will growing cold

15. This gospel of the Kingdom being preached in all the world as a witness to all nations and then the end will come.

For the first time since the early church this verse about the gospel of the Kingdom being preached in all the world as a witness is coming to pass. There are more Christians alive in the world now than all previous 2,000 years of church history combined. The gospel of the Kingdom is being not only 'told' but 'witnessed' through the power of the Holy Spirit performing miracles, signs and wonders. The true power and demonstrating ('witness') of God's kingdom is at last beginning to explode in all the world. Entire nations are being radically transformed by the presence of God's kingdom through the life of His people. This is the greatest day in the history of Christianity! This is the greatest hour of the church and God's people in all the world. Tens of thousands of people are coming to the saving knowledge of Christ every day around the world. China now has over a hundred and fifty million believers. Christian ministries are beginning to partner with those from different denominations and groups to unite together for the sake of world evangelism. That has never happened like it is beginning to now. The last days are here now. The 1948 restoration of Israel to a nation after over 2,000 years is the centerpiece of prophetic discourse covering the last days.

Ezekiel 36:24-38 (NKJV)

For I will take you from among the nations, gather you out of all countries, and bring you into your own land. Then I will sprinkle clean water on you, and you shall be clean; I will cleanse you from all your filthiness and from all your idols. I will give you a new heart and put a new spirit within you; I will take the heart of stone out of your flesh and give you a heart of flesh. I will put My Spirit within you and cause you to walk in My statutes, and you will keep My judgments and do them. Then you shall dwell in the land that I gave to your fathers; you shall be My people, and I will be your God. I will deliver you from all your uncleannesses. I will call for the grain and multiply it, and bring no famine upon you. And I will multiply the fruit of your trees and the increase of your fields, so that you need never again bear the reproach of famine among the nations. Then you will remember your evil ways and your deeds that were not good; and you will loathe yourselves in your own sight, for your iniquities and your abominations. Not for your sake do I do this," says the Lord GOD, "let it be known to you. Be ashamed and confounded for your own ways, O house of Israel!"

'Thus says the Lord GOD: "On the day that I cleanse you from all your iniquities, I will also enable you to dwell in the cities, and the ruins shall be rebuilt. The desolate land shall be tilled instead of lying desolate in the sight of all who pass by. So they will say, 'This land that was desolate has become like the garden of Eden; and the wasted, desolate, and ruined cities are now fortified and inhabited.' Then the nations which are left all around you shall know that I, the LORD, have rebuilt the ruined places and planted what was desolate. I, the LORD, have spoken it, and I will do it."

'Thus says the Lord GOD: "I will also let the house of Israel inquire of Me to do this for them: I will increase their men like a flock. Like a flock offered as holy sacrifices, like the flock at Jerusalem on its feast days, so shall the ruined cities be filled with flocks of men. Then they shall know that I am the LORD.""'

Ezekiel 37:21-22 (NKJV)
"Then say to them, 'Thus says the Lord GOD: "Surely I will take the children of Israel from among the nations, wherever they have gone, and will gather them from every side and bring them into their own land; and I will make them one nation in the land, on the mountains of Israel; and one king shall be king over them all; they shall no longer be two nations, nor shall they ever be divided into two kingdoms again.

Ezekiel 34:13 (NKJV)
And I will bring them out from the peoples and gather them from the countries,

and will bring them to their own land; I will feed them on the mountains of Israel, in the valleys and in all the inhabited places of the country.

Jeremiah 23:3 (NKJV)
"But I will gather the remnant of My flock out of all countries where I have driven them, and bring them back to their folds; and they shall be fruitful and increase.

Jeremiah 23:8 NKJV)
. . . but, 'As the LORD lives who brought up and led the descendants of the house of Israel from the north country and from all the countries where I had driven them.' And they shall dwell in their own land."

Jeremiah 32:37 (NKJV)
Behold, I will gather them out of all countries where I have driven them in My anger, in My fury, and in great wrath; I will bring them back to this place, and I will cause them to dwell safely.

Deuteronomy 30:3 (NKJV)
. . . that the LORD your God will bring you back from captivity, and have compassion on you, and gather you again from all the nations where the LORD your God has scattered you.

In 1967 the ancient holy city of Jerusalem was restored to Israel as the Word of God prophetically declares.

Jeremiah 33:10-11 (NKJV)
"Thus says the LORD: 'Again there shall be heard in this place—of which you say, "It is desolate, without man and without beast"—in the cities of Judah, in the streets of Jerusalem that are desolate, without man and without inhabitant and without beast, the voice of joy and the voice of gladness, the voice of the bridegroom and the voice of the bride, the voice of those who will say: "Praise the LORD of hosts, for the LORD is good, for His mercy endures forever"— and of those who will bring the sacrifice of praise into the house of the LORD. For I will cause the captives of the land to return as at the first,' says the LORD.

Zechariah 8:1-7 (NKJV)

Again the word of the LORD of hosts came, saying, "Thus says the LORD of hosts: 'I am zealous for Zion with great zeal; with great fervor I am zealous for her.'

"Thus says the LORD: 'I will return to Zion, and dwell in the midst of Jerusalem. Jerusalem shall be called the City of Truth, the Mountain of the LORD of hosts, the Holy Mountain.'

"Thus says the LORD of hosts: 'Old men and old women shall again sit in the streets of Jerusalem, each one with his staff in his hand because of great age.

The streets of the city shall be full of boys and girls playing in its streets.'

"Thus says the LORD of hosts: 'If it is marvelous in the eyes of the remnant of this people in these days, will it also be marvelous in My eyes?' says the LORD of hosts.

"Thus says the LORD of hosts: 'Behold, I will save My people from the land of the east and from the land of the west;

I will bring them back, and they shall dwell in the midst of Jerusalem. They shall be My people and I will be their God, in truth and righteousness.'

Further major last day prophecies are given to us related to several important events:

1. A Great Falling Away of Believers

I believe this is now seen in the backsliding of formerly Christian Europe, which now represents the most unreached continent in the world today. Others believe that this falling away will occur by a great rebellion against God during the great tribulation (the church already being raptured).

1 Timothy 4:1 (NKJV)

Now the Spirit expressly says that in latter times some will depart from the faith, giving heed to deceiving spirits and doctrines of demons...

2. Antichrist

The spirit of the antichrist has wreaked havoc in the world for thousands of years. Many false prophets and many other deceiving and oppressing figures have gone throughout history. I believe though, there will be an actual person who rises to world power during the last days that will be the fulfillment of biblical prophecy

II Thessalonians 2:3-12 (NKJV)

Let no one deceive you by any means; for that Day will not come unless the falling away comes first, and the man of sin is revealed, the son of perdition, who opposes and exalts himself above all that is called God or that is worshiped, so that he sits as God in the temple of God, showing himself that he is God.

Do you not remember that when I was still with you I told you these things? And now you know what is restraining, that he may be revealed in his own time. For the mystery of lawlessness is already at work; only He who now restrains will do so until He is taken out of the way. And then the lawless one will be revealed, whom the Lord will consume with the breath of His mouth and destroy with the brightness of His coming. The coming of the lawless one is according to the working of Satan, with all power, signs, and lying wonders, and with all unrighteous deception among those who perish, because they did not receive the love of the truth, that they might be saved. And for this reason God will send them strong delusion, that they should believe the lie, that they all may be condemned who did not believe the truth but had pleasure in unrighteousness.

II Thessalonians 2:3-12 (MSG)

Before that day comes, a couple of things have to happen. First, the Apostasy. Second, the debut of the Anarchist, a real dog of Satan. He'll defy and then take over every so-called god or altar. Having cleared away the opposition, he'll then set himself up in God's Temple as "God Almighty." Don't you remember me going over all this in detail when I was with you? Are your memories that short?

You'll also remember that I told you the Anarchist is being held back until just the right time. That doesn't mean that the spirit of anarchy is not now at work. It is, secretly and underground. But the time will come when the Anarchist will no longer be held back, but will be let loose. But don't worry. The Master Jesus will be right on his heels and blow him away. The Master appears and—puff!—the Anarchist is out of there.

The Anarchist's coming is all Satan's work. All his power and signs and miracles are fake, evil sleight of hand that plays to the gallery of those who hate the truth that could save them. And since they're so obsessed with evil, God rubs their noses in it—gives them what they want. Since they refuse to trust truth, they're banished to their chosen world of lies and illusions.

Daniel 7:25 (NKJV)

He shall speak pompous words against the Most High, shall persecute the saints of the Most High, and shall intend to change times and law. Then the saints shall be given into his hand for a time and times and half a time.

Daniel 8:23-25 (NKJV)

"And in the latter time of their kingdom, when the transgressors have reached their fullness, a king shall arise, having fierce features, who understands sinister schemes. His power shall be mighty, but not by his own power; he shall destroy fearfully, and shall prosper and thrive; he shall destroy the mighty, and also the holy people.

"Through his cunning he shall cause deceit to prosper under his rule; and he shall exalt himself in his heart. He shall destroy many in their prosperity. He shall even rise against the Prince of princes; but he shall be broken without human means.

Daniel 8:23-25 (MSG)

"'As their kingdoms cool down and rebellions heat up, a king will show up, hard-faced, a master trickster. His power will swell enormously.

"He'll talk big, high-handedly, doing whatever he pleases, knocking off heroes and holy ones left and right. He'll plot and scheme to make crime flourish—and oh, how it will flourish! He'll think he's invincible and get rid of anyone who gets in his way. But when he takes on the Prince of all princes, he'll be smashed to bits—but not by human hands.

Daniel 11:36 (NKJV)

"Then the king shall do according to his own will: he shall exalt and magnify himself above every god, shall speak blasphemies against the God of gods, and shall prosper till the wrath has been accomplished; for what has been determined shall be done.

Revelation 13:1-6 (NKJV)

Then I stood on the sand of the sea. And I saw a beast rising up out of the sea, having seven heads and ten horns, and on his horns ten crowns, and on his heads a blasphemous name. Now the beast which I saw was like a leopard, his feet were like the feet of a bear, and his mouth like the mouth of a lion. The dragon gave him his power, his throne, and great authority. And I saw one of his heads as if it had been mortally wounded, and his deadly wound was healed. And all the world marveled and followed the beast. So they worshiped the dragon who gave authority to the beast; and they worshiped the beast, saying, "Who is like the beast? Who is able to make war with him?"

And he was given a mouth speaking great things and blasphemies, and he was given authority to continue for forty-two months. Then he opened his mouth in blasphemy against God, to blaspheme His name, His tabernacle, and those who dwell in heaven.

The antichrist will first arise as a man of peace for the nations. He could be the one who brokers a temporary truce in the Middle East before his true nature emerges to attempt to destroy Israel. He will have the power of a great deceptor and many will be captured by his work of evil. The antichrist will establish an image of himself and order everyone to worship it.

3. The False Prophet - A full partner in power and demonic deception with the antichrist.

Revelation 16:13-14 (NKJV)

And I saw three unclean spirits like frogs coming out of the mouth of the dragon, out of the mouth of the beast, and out of the mouth of the false prophet. For they are spirits of demons, performing signs, which go out to the kings of the earth and of the whole world, to gather them to the battle of that great day of God Almighty.

Revelation 13:11, 14 (NKJV)

Then I saw another beast coming up out of the earth, and he had two horns like a lamb and spoke like a dragon.

And he deceives those who dwell on the earth by those signs which he was granted to do in the sight of the beast, telling those who dwell on the earth to make an image to the beast who was wounded by the sword and lived.

Revelation 19:20 (NKJV)

Then the beast was captured, and with him the false prophet who worked signs in his presence, by which he deceived those who received the mark of the beast and those who worshiped his image. These two were cast alive into the lake of fire burning with brimstone.

Revelation 20:10 (NKJV)

The devil, who deceived them, was cast into the lake of fire and brimstone where the beast and the false prophet are. And they will be tormented day and night forever and ever.

The false prophet is Satan's counterfeit to the Holy Spirit. He has the ability to perform false miracles and signs that will fascinate and deceive many to accept his message and that of his partner, the antichrist. Together they marshal a last day revolt against God himself and are suddenly defeated and cast into the lake of fire.

4. The Great Tribulation - A period of time across the whole earth with the greatest pressure, persecution, fear and oppression in human history.

Matthew 24:21-22 (NKJV)

For then there will be great tribulation, such as has not been since the beginning of the world until this time, no, nor ever shall be. And unless those days were shortened, no flesh would be saved; but for the elect's sake those days will be shortened.

Matthew 24:21-22 (MSG)

"This is going to be trouble on a scale beyond what the world has ever seen, or will see again. If these days of trouble were left to run their course, nobody would make it. But on account of God's chosen people, the trouble will be cut short.

Matthew 24:21-22 (NLT)

For there will be greater anguish than at any time since the world began. And it will never be so great again. In fact, unless that time of calamity is shortened, not a single person will survive. But it will be shortened for the sake of God's chosen ones.

God's people will witness God's delivering power during this time.

Revelation 3:10 (NKJV)
Because you have kept My command to persevere, I also will keep you from the hour of trial which shall come upon the whole world, to test those who dwell on the earth.

Revelation 7:14 (NKJV)
And I said to him, "Sir, you know."
So he said to me, "These are the ones who come out of the great tribulation, and washed their robes and made them white in the blood of the Lamb.

It is my opinion that the scriptures are purposely uncertain concerning the actual time line of the great tribulation. Depending on their belief, there are several views concerning this event. Many believe the Rapture (taking of the church) will happen before the tribulation. This is called a pre-tribulation view. Others believe the Rapture will take place midway through the great tribulation, this is called the mid-tribulation view. Others believe the Rapture will transpire after the tribulation, this is called the post-tribulation view.

5. The Millennium
This is the 1,000 year reign of Christ on the earth in the New Jerusalem after the Rapture and the Second Coming. Those believers who were raptured will come back to rule with their conquering king. There are three major positions on this in Christianity.

A. Premillennial view
Views the 1,000 years as a literal period of time that is initiated by the second coming of Christ. The 1,000 year reign of Christ with His church ends with the final judgment and destruction of Satan after a brief period of activity.

II Peter 2:4 (NKJV)

For if God did not spare the angels who sinned, but cast them down to hell and delivered them into chains of darkness, to be reserved for judgment;

Jude 1:6 (NKJV)

And the angels who did not keep their proper domain, but left their own abode, He has reserved in everlasting chains under darkness for the judgment of the great day...

B. Postmillennial view

This interpretation holds that the 1,000 year period of peace on earth is ushered in by the church. The second coming of Christ is not until the end of this thousand year period. Satan is unleashed at the end of this period but is defeated by the return of Christ who comes to reign forever.

C. Amillennial view

Takes this 1,000 year period as only symbolic of the amount of time between the first and second coming of Christ. This millennium is represented by the Kingdom of God reigning in the hearts of God's church, called the Church Age. The second coming of Christ ends this age.

6. Final Judgment- The day when every person stands before God.

The believers' final judgment- The Bema Seat

Romans 14:10-12 (NKJV)

But why do you judge your brother? Or why do you show contempt for your brother? For we shall all stand before the judgment seat of Christ. For it is written: "As I live, says the LORD, every knee shall bow to Me, and every tongue shall confess to God." So then each of us shall give account of himself to God.

II Corinthians 5:9-11 (NKJV)

Therefore we make it our aim, whether present or absent, to be well pleasing to Him. For we must all appear before the judgment seat of Christ, that each one may receive the things done in the body, according to what he has done, whether good or bad. Knowing, therefore, the terror of the Lord, we persuade men; but we are well known to God, and I also trust are well known in your consciences.

Revelation 11:18 (NKJV)
The nations were angry, and Your wrath has come, and the time of the dead, that they should be judged, and that You should reward Your servants the prophets and the saints, and those who fear Your name, small and great, and should destroy those who destroy the earth."

I John 4:17 (NKJV)
Love has been perfected among us in this: that we may have boldness in the day of judgment; because as He is, so are we in this world.

I John 4:17 (MSG)
God is love. When we take up permanent residence in a life of love, we live in God and God lives in us. This way, love has the run of the house, becomes at home and mature in us, so that we're free of worry on Judgment Day—our standing in the world is identical with Christ's.

The place of judgment for believers has nothing to do with eternal life in heaven. This is the place where we all will give an accounting to our Lord about how we stewarded His grace and gifts in our lifetime. What did we do with what we were given? What kind of life did we exemplify? Were we a lukewarm Christian or an on fire one? Did we find and fulfill our kingdom destiny and purpose as His children? Christ taught about this day of personal accountability to God in two different parables.

Matthew 25:1-30 (MSG)
"God's kingdom is like ten young virgins who took oil lamps and went out to greet the bridegroom. Five were silly and five were smart. The silly virgins took lamps, but no extra oil. The smart virgins took jars of oil to feed their lamps. The bridegroom didn't show up when they expected him, and they all fell asleep.

"In the middle of the night someone yelled out, 'He's here! The bridegroom's here! Go out and greet him!'

"The ten virgins got up and got their lamps ready. The silly virgins said to the smart ones, 'Our lamps are going out; lend us some of your oil.'

"They answered, 'There might not be enough to go around; go buy your own.'

"They did, but while they were out buying oil, the bridegroom arrived. When everyone who was there to greet him had gone into the wedding feast, the door was locked.

"Much later, the other virgins, the silly ones, showed up and knocked on the door, saying, 'Master, we're here. Let us in.'

"He answered, 'Do I know you? I don't think I know you.'

"So stay alert. You have no idea when he might arrive.

"It's also like a man going off on an extended trip. He called his servants together and delegated responsibilities. To one he gave five thousand dollars, to another two thousand, to a third one thousand, depending on their abilities. Then he left. Right off, the first servant went to work and doubled his master's investment. The second did the same. But the man with the single thousand dug a hole and carefully buried his master's money.

"After a long absence, the master of those three servants came back and settled up with them. The one given five thousand dollars showed him how he had doubled his investment. His master commended him: 'Good work! You did your job well. From now on be my partner.'

"The servant with the two thousand showed how he also had doubled his master's investment. His master commended him: 'Good work! You did your job well. From now on be my partner.'

"The servant given one thousand said, 'Master, I know you have high standards and hate careless ways, that you demand the best and make no allowances for error. I was afraid I might disappoint you, so I found a good hiding place and secured your money. Here it is, safe and sound down to the last cent.'

"The master was furious. 'That's a terrible way to live! It's criminal to live cautiously like that! If you knew I was after the best, why did you do less than the least? The least you could have done would have been to invest the sum with the bankers, where at least I would have gotten a little interest.

"'Take the thousand and give it to the one who risked the most. And get rid of this "play-it-safe" who won't go out on a limb. Throw him out into utter darkness.'

Both these parables speak of the rewards of being prepared and faithful with our lives as His children and vice versa as the punishment for being indifferent and complacent with the blessings and gifts He has given us. The terms of this chapter are a picture of the great regret many will have when they realize how much of their life was wasted in missed opportunity to what God's will was for them.

THE UNSAVED FINAL JUDGMENT

Hebrews 9:27 (NKJV)

And as it is appointed for men to die once, but after this the judgment,

II Timothy 4:1 (NKJV)

I charge you therefore before God and the Lord Jesus Christ, who will judge the living and the dead at His appearing and His kingdom:

II Peter 2:9 (NKJV)

. . . then the Lord knows how to deliver the godly out of temptations and to reserve the unjust under punishment for the day of judgment,

II Peter 3:7 (NKJV)

But the heavens and the earth which are now preserved by the same word, are reserved for fire until the day of judgment and perdition of ungodly men.

Hebrews 6:2 (NKJV)

. . . of the doctrine of baptisms, of laying on of hands, of resurrection of the dead, and of eternal judgment.

Hebrews 10:27 (NKJV)

. . . but a certain fearful expectation of judgment, and fiery indignation which will devour the adversaries.

Hebrews 10:31

It is a fearful thing to fall into the hands of the living God.

Revelation 20:11-15 (NKJV)

Then I saw a great white throne and Him who sat on it, from whose face the earth and the heaven fled away. And there was found no place for them. And I saw the dead, small and great, standing before God, and books were opened. And another book was opened, which is the Book of Life. And the dead were judged according to their works, by the things which were written in the books. The sea gave up the dead who were in it, and Death and Hades delivered up the dead who were in them. And they were judged, each one according to his works. Then Death and Hades were cast into the lake of fire. This is the second death. And anyone not found written in the Book of Life was cast into the lake of fire.

The description of the day of judgment to the unsaved is heartbreaking and horrific. Hell is not a myth! It is real and we as believers must be compelled to deliver as many souls from that horrible destination as possible. Jesus came to rescue and redeem all mankind from the penalty of our sins, death and eternal separation from God in hell. Jesus said there are only two kinds of people, those who believe and those who don't.

Mark 16:16 (NKJV)
He who believes and is baptized will be saved; but he who does not believe will be condemned.

Let us make it our life mission to win as many souls for Christ as we possibly can.

James 5:19-20 (NKJV)
Brethren, if anyone among you wanders from the truth, and someone turns him back, let him know that he who turns a sinner from the error of his way will save a soul[a] from death and cover a multitude of sins.

The Old Testament book of Daniel is filled with a rich prophetic portrait of the last days. In this book there are at least eight last day events foretold to us. With all end-time prophecies, experts and others are studying, trying to interpret these and other last day prophecy with the Bible, greatly educated and well-meaning believers can and do hold varying and divergent opinions and beliefs about these mysterious prophecies. To successfully navigate this we must purposely remain in the spirit of unity towards one another, refusing to allow any disagreement concerning the very subjective study of last day prophecy to cause a spirit of division or judgment to sprout up in our hearts. There is no other area of Christian doctrine and biblical study that has as much mystery and theological uncertainty as the study of the last days (called 'eschatology' in theology), the "study of last things."

DANIEL'S 8 LAST DAY PROPHECIES

1. The second coming of Christ will occur before the millennium period. (Dan. 2:31-37, 44-45, 7:13-14)
2. The Lord will set up His Kingdom on earth. (Dan. 2:44-45, 7:26-27)
3. Four great empires shall reign as revealed in Nebuchadnezzar's dream: Babylonian, Medo-Persian, Greek, and Roman (Dan. 2:37-40)
4. The last kingdom, Rome, will return in the form of a multi-national confederacy of which the antichrist will emerge from. (Dan. 7:8, 20-21, 8:23)
5. The antichrist and the false prophet are actual persons and not merely systems. (Dan. 7:3-8, 20-26, 9:27, 11:36-40
6. God will continue to relate and deal with the nation of Israel. (Dan. 9:20-27)
7. Israel is God's prophetic time clock for last day events. (Dan. 9:24)
8. The antichrist and the false prophet will rise to world influence and dominion during the last week of Daniel's seventy weeks of years. At the end of the 'week' after the Great Tribulation Jesus will return to establish His Kingdom.

CHAPTER 6
QUESTIONS AND ANSWERS

1. What are the 5 things that will occur when Christ comes back to earth from I Thess. 4:13-18? _____, _____, _____, _____, and _____

2. The Bible says that all believers are to live with the _____ _____ of our Lord's soon appearing.

3. The Bible says this 'day of the Lord' (the day of the second coming of Christ) will come ____ __ _____ ____ _____ _____.

4. There are more Christians alive in the world today than in all _____ ____ ____ ____ _____ _____.

5. The centerpiece of end time prophetic discourse was the _____ _____ _____ _____ _____.

6. There are five important last day events prophesied in scriptures. What are they? _____ _____ _____ _____ _____

7. _____ is not a myth. It is real and we as believers must be _____ ____ _____as many souls from that horrible destination.

8. There is no other area of Christian doctrine and biblical study that has as much mystery and theological uncertainty as the _____ _____ _____ _____.

9. Greatly educated and well-meaning believers can and do hold _____ _____ ____ _____ about these mysterious prophecies.

10. The study of last things is called _____.

7 THE WORD OF GOD

At the very core and foundation of our Christian faith and doctrine is the absolute belief that the Bible is the Word of God. Not that the Bible merely includes or records some of God's Word, but that the entirety of the 66 books of the Bible, every word from beginning to end, is the Word of God. The Bible says this about itself in II Timothy 3:15-17 (NKJV).

. . . and that from childhood you have known the Holy Scriptures, which are able to make you wise for salvation through faith which is in Christ Jesus.

All Scripture is given by inspiration of God, and is profitable for doctrine, for reproof, for correction, for instruction in righteousness, that the man of God may be complete, thoroughly equipped for every good work.

II Timothy 3:15-17 (The MSG)
Stick with what you learned and believed, sure of the integrity of your teachers—why, you took in the sacred Scriptures with your mother's milk! There's nothing like the written Word of God for showing you the way to salvation through faith in Christ Jesus. Every part of Scripture is God-breathed and useful one way or another—showing us truth, exposing our rebellion, correcting our mistakes, training

us to live God's way. Through the Word we are put together and shaped up for the tasks God has for us.

II Timothy 3:15-17 (AMP)

And how from your childhood you have had a knowledge of and been acquainted with the sacred Writings, which are able to instruct you and give you the understanding for salvation which comes through faith in Christ Jesus [through the leaning of the entire human personality on God in Christ Jesus in absolute trust and confidence in His power, wisdom, and goodness].

Every Scripture is God-breathed (given by His inspiration) and profitable for instruction, for reproof and conviction of sin, for correction of error and discipline in obedience, [and] for training in righteousness (in holy living, in conformity to God's will in thought, purpose, and action),

So that the man of God may be complete and proficient, well fitted and thoroughly equipped for every good work.

THE DIVINE INSPIRATION OF THE SCRIPTURES

All scripture is given to us by the 'inspiration of God'. The Greek word for 'inspired of God' is "theopneustos" which literally means "God breathed". The Bible is not the past history of ancient peoples or a compilation of various human stories, myths and ideas. The Bible is the inspired Word of God. The Bible does not represent the greatest and highest expression of human or intellectual enlightenment, but all scripture, the entirety of the Bible is 'breathed' from God Himself to us. The process by which God accomplished this is revealed in II Peter 1:20-21 (NKJV).

. . . knowing this first, that no prophecy of Scripture is of any private interpretation, for prophecy never came by the will of man, but holy men of God spoke as they were moved by the Holy Spirit.

II Peter 1:20-21 (MSG)

The main thing to keep in mind here is that no prophecy of Scripture is a matter of private opinion. And why? Because it's not something concocted in the human heart. Prophecy resulted when the Holy Spirit prompted men and women to speak God's Word.

II Peter 1:20-21 (AMP)

[Yet] first [you must] understand this, that no prophecy of Scripture is [a matter] of any personal or private or special interpretation (loosening, solving).

For no prophecy ever originated because some man willed it [to do so--it never came by human impulse], but men spoke from God who were borne along (moved and impelled) by the Holy Spirit.

II Peter 1:20-21 (NLT)

Above all, you must realize that no prophecy in Scripture ever came from the prophet's own understanding, or from human initiative. No, those prophets were moved by the Holy Spirit, and they spoke from God.

The scriptures are not the opinions, thoughts or concepts of mens' minds and beliefs. Men wrote the scriptures as they were 'moved by the Holy Spirit.' God inspired the authors of the scriptures. He used their human intellect, ability, education and gifts. These writers were placed under the complete control and divine inspiration of the Holy Spirit to perfectly accomplish His will in the revelation of His Word to mankind. This is what separates the Bible from every other book and teaching. The Bible is authored by God himself who revealed His Word in divine inspiration to men, who recorded it for us. This truth is invaluable, irreplaceable and absolutely essential for you to securely grasp and understand. In all the world there are many books that may contain some truly inspired thoughts and truth, but there is only one book that is wholly and perfectly divinely inspired in its entirety. That book is the Bible, the Word of God. Without settling this in your heart, you will never be able to truly know God and the amazing truth that His Word alone contains for your life. Everything we are to learn about God in this life can only be safely and truthfully discovered through the study and revelation of the scriptures, which in themselves are the complete revelation of God to man. The faithful study and application of the scriptures will allow us to be this person.

"That the man of God may be complete (mature, Christ-like, fully grown, everything God created you to be in Jesus), thoroughly equipped for every good work," or as the message version declares:

"Through the world we are put together and shaped up for the tasks God has for us."

"Every part of scripture is God-breathed and useful in one way or another- showing us truth, exposing our rebellion, correcting our mistakes, training us to live Gods way."

The description of the Bible being divinely inspired in every single word is called the "plenary verbal inspiration of the scriptures." This is what we as followers of Christ believe is the absolute truth. This belief grants us access by faith into the fullness of God's blessings, will and kingdom that His word unveils to our lives.

THE PERFECTION OF GOD'S WORD

Psalm 19:7-11 (NKJV)

The law of the LORD is perfect, converting the soul; the testimony of the LORD is sure, making wise the simple;

The statutes of the LORD are right, rejoicing the heart; the commandment of the LORD is pure, enlightening the eyes;

The fear of the LORD is clean, enduring forever; the judgments of the LORD are true and righteous altogether.

More to be desired are they than gold, yea, than much fine gold;

Sweeter also than honey and the honeycomb.

Moreover by them Your servant is warned, and in keeping them there is great reward.

The phrase 'law of the Lord' used here is synonymous with 'the Word of God.' The Word of God is declared here as being perfect. It is perfect in its authorship, accuracy and absoluteness. It is completely perfect in its revelation, and thusly, it is complete in its trustworthiness and dependability. We use two different words to describe the perfection of God's Word. The first is Inerrant (perfect).

The Inerrancy of God's Word

The foundation for biblical inerrancy is shown to us in the miraculous delivery of God's Word throughout the ages beginning with the individual writers the Holy Spirit wrote the scriptures through. Inerrancy means that in the original manuscripts of each book of the Bible there was no error or mistake. No factual, historical or theological distortions, deceptions or imperfections. The Bible was transmitted to us inerrant (perfectly).

Not only were the original ancient manuscripts faultless, but the subsequent retransmissions (the copies or the manuscripts made down through time) were accomplished perfectly (inerrant). In all of history there has never been such a carefully meticulous process as what even secular, non-religious scholars of history and literature acknowledge occurred in the copying of the scriptures. Inerrancy means what we now read in our Bibles is exactly or perfectly what God revealed by divine inspiration to the writers of the scriptures.

The Infallible Word of God

The second aspect of the perfection of the scriptures is what we call Infallible. This means the Bible is completely unfailing in its promises and truth. It is the expression of God's absolute truth to us in its every promise and revelation. Because of that, we can receive it with absolute faith and trust in its unfailing (infallible) ability. God is incapable of lying as these writers attest.

Titus 1:2 (NKJV)
. . . in hope of eternal life which God, who cannot lie, promised before time began,

Hebrews 6:18 (NKJV)
. . . that by two immutable things, in which it is impossible for God to lie, we might have strong consolation, who have fled for refuge to lay hold of the hope set before us.

Numbers 23:19 (NKJV)
"God is not a man, that He should lie, Nor a son of man, that He should repent. Has He said, and will He not do? Or has He spoken, and will He not make it good? His word is an eternally settled truth for us to put our complete confidence and faith in its reliability.

Psalm 119:89-91 (NKJV)
Forever, O LORD, Your word is settled in heaven.
    Your faithfulness endures to all generations; You established the earth, and it abides.
    They continue this day according to Your ordinances, for all are Your servants.

His word to us is timeless. Everything in the world around us is in constant cycles or change but God's word is unchanging and eternal.

Mark 13:31 (NKJV)
Heaven and earth will pass away, but My words will by no means pass away.

Mark 13:31 (MSG)
Sky and earth will wear out; my words won't wear out.

Mark 13:31 (NLT)
Heaven and earth will disappear, but my words will never disappear.

Isaiah 40:8 (NKJV)
The grass withers, the flower fades, but the word of our God stands forever."

Isaiah 40:8 (MSG)
True, the grass withers and the wildflowers fade, but our God's Word stands firm and forever."

Any and every personal revelation we or anyone else receives and claims to be from or about God is to be examined through the lens and truth of the Holy Scriptures. If it does not line up or agree with the Bible, then it is not to be received as truth. All such experiences or revelations that are in biblical agreement that anyone receives are fine, but they will never rise to the level of truth and divine inspiration that is uniquely expressed in the Word of God, the Bible.

THE BIBLE IS FILLED WITH GOD'S LIFE AND POWER

Hebrews 4:12 (MSG)
God means what he says. What he says goes. His powerful Word is sharp as a surgeon's scalpel, cutting through everything, whether doubt or defense, laying us open to listen and obey.

Hebrews 4:12 (NLT)
For the word of God is alive and powerful. It is sharper than the sharpest two-edged

sword, cutting between soul and spirit, between joint and marrow. It exposes our innermost thoughts and desires.

Hebrews 4:12 (AMP)
For the Word that God speaks is alive and full of power [making it active, operative, energizing, and effective]; it is sharper than any two-edged sword, penetrating to the dividing line of the breath of life (soul) and [the immortal] spirit, and of joints and marrow [of the deepest parts of our nature], exposing and sifting and analyzing and judging the very thoughts and purposes of the heart.

Hebrews 4:12 (NKJV)
For the word of God is living and powerful, and sharper than any two-edged sword, piercing even to the division of soul and spirit, and of joints and marrow, and is a discerner of the thoughts and intents of the heart.

The scriptures are not a mere collection of various truths and teachings about God or the simple record of what God said. The Bible is the living, powerful, dynamic and life-transforming Word of God. It's alive with God's very life and nature. It's dynamic and powerful and capable of changing anyone who opens their heart to its promises. It penetrates to the very core of our lives and there in the foundation of our lives and person, there in the depths of our human and sinful nature, the Word of God, like a skilled surgeon's scalpel, performs the divine surgery of transforming our very nature by its presence. There is no person, problem or circumstance that the living Word of God cannot change.

Isaiah 55:10-11 (NKJV)
"For as the rain comes down, and the snow from heaven, and do not return there, but water the earth, and make it bring forth and bud, that it may give seed to the sower and bread to the eater,
So shall My word be that goes forth from My mouth; it shall not return to Me void, but it shall accomplish what I please, and it shall prosper in the thing for which I sent it.

Isaiah 55:10-11 (NLT)

"The rain and snow come down from the heavens and stay on the ground to water the earth. They cause the grain to grow, producing seed for the farmer and bread for the hungry.

It is the same with my word. I send it out, and it always produces fruit. It will accomplish all I want it to, and it will prosper everywhere I send it.

God's Word never fails! When it is properly received, watered and maintained, the seed of His word always produces the harvest it has declared. It is God's very life and power that each promise of the scriptures contains. His word is incapable of being fruitless or unfulfilled in our lives when we believe and act on it. The seed (Word of God) is always perfect; the soil (our hearts) is where we must learn to cultivate an environment conducive to growing the seed (the promise of God becoming a reality in our life).

BECOME A PASSIONATE STUDENT OF GOD'S WORD

II Timothy 2:15 (NKJV)

Be diligent to present yourself approved to God, a worker who does not need to be ashamed, rightly dividing the word of truth.

II Timothy 2:15 (AMP)

Study and be eager and do your utmost to present yourself to God approved (tested by trial), a workman who has no cause to be ashamed, correctly analyzing and accurately dividing [rightly handling and skillfully teaching] the Word of Truth.

The Bible will benefit you to the degree of your study and knowledge of it. It is the complete revelation of God's will for your life. If you don't know what's in the will (like someone leaving a fortune for you in their 'will'), then you will never experience the heavenly blessing.

Hosea 4:6(a)

My people are destroyed for lack of knowledge. Because you have rejected knowledge,

What we don't know doesn't just keep us from receiving God's grace and blessing as revealed in the Holy Scriptures, it brings destruction. Ignorance of Gods will, as perfectly and completely revealed in the scriptures, will bring tremendous devastation into your life.

The motto of the mission of the F.B.I is "the truth shall set you free" which is a portion of Scripture spoken to us by Jesus, who is the 'Living Word.'.

> John 8:31-32 (NKJV)
> Then Jesus said to those Jews who believed Him, "If you abide in My word, you are My disciples indeed. And you shall know the truth, and the truth shall make you free."

There are at least three great revelations for us to see from these verses:

First Jesus defines that his true disciples are those who "continue in His word."

That's what discipleship is for you and me, continually with Christ in unbroken fellowship and obedience to His word. We continue by allowing the truth of His word into our lives and letting it change us from the inside out. We continue with Christ by refusing to reject unwanted or unessential truth we find personally difficult, challenging or uncomfortable. (Example: learning from our parents to eat vegetables and other food that is good for our health, but not necessarily good to the taste). Our continuing with Christ as His disciples means we eat (welcome and receive) whatever meal (teaching from Scripture) He chooses to feed us. As disciples we can't view our lives as possessing authority over His will - kind of like a person who walks through a long food buffet, picking and choosing what they want and skipping what they don't. As disciples we joyously, humbly and obediently welcome the meal of His word that He has chosen to prepare to feed us.

Secondly, the borrowed motto of the F.B.I. "the truth shall set us free" is only part of what Christ said, and because it is in part, it is incomplete and ultimately then not true.

The truth does not set us free; it is only the truth that we know that has the power to set us free! Jesus said that we would know the truth, and truth we know would then do its powerful work in setting us free. The truth is here now, yet billions of souls remain in bondage and slavery to sin, sickness and Satan's oppression. That's because although the truth is here, they either don't know it or have rejected it. The Greek word Christ used for know is 'ginosko' which means "knowledge that has begun and then progresses until it produces the desired result." It means to perceive, understand and realize. It is not merely intellectual knowledge (head knowledge), but truth that ultimately becomes personal experience.

Thirdly, Christ promises all mankind that as we continue with Him in discipleship, we then are qualified to know the truth and are confident the truth will always set us free!

The Greek word for 'set us free' is eleutheroo which means "to liberate, deliver, set free." It comes from the word eleutheros which means "to be unrestrained (to go at pleasure), to be a citizen, not a slave." The slavery of our lives to sin and conformity to the world is wonderfully broken off of us like an ancient slave who was shackled and granted full rights and privileges of a citizen. This heaven-sent freedom is emphasized to us from Christ in the proceeding verses.

John 8:36 (NKJV)
Therefore if the Son makes you free, you shall be free indeed.

John 8:36 (MSG)
So if the Son sets you free, you are free through and through.

John 8:36 (AMP)
So if the Son liberates you [makes you free men], then you are really and unquestionably free.

Christ has purchased our lives complete freedom in His victorious redemption. That victory is delivered to us in the powerful promises of the Holy Scriptures. The heavenly truth of those great promises will bring to us the full freedom and victory of our glorious Savior. That freedom He gives us is so powerful that nothing can take it from us. We are truly 'free indeed' through and through in Jesus.

FAITH COMES BY HEARING GOD'S WORD

As infants our parents fed us milk and then as we grew, baby food and as we grew more, eventually adult food. Even now, when we are fully grown, we still require food for nourishment of strength and life. Just as our bodies need food and without it cannot live, so as believers, do our spirits need food. The food that nourishes, strengthens and gives life to our spirit is the Word of God. Jesus said in Matthew 4:4 (NKJV):

But He answered and said, "It is written, 'Man shall not live by bread alone, but by every word that proceeds from the mouth of God.'"

Matthew 4:4 (MSG)
Jesus answered by quoting Deuteronomy: "It takes more than bread to stay alive. It takes a steady stream of words from God's mouth."

Matthew 4:4 (AMP)
But He replied, It has been written, Man shall not live and be upheld and sustained by bread alone, but by every word that comes forth from the mouth of God.

Matthew 4:4 (NLT)
But Jesus told him, "No! The Scriptures say, 'People do not live by bread alone, but by every word that comes from the mouth of God.'

Just as newborn babies cry out when they are hungry, the spirit of believers cries out for the food of the word of God.

I Peter 2:2 (NKJV)
. . . as newborn babes, desire the pure milk of the word, that you may grow thereby,

I Peter 2:2 (NLT)
Like newborn babies, you must crave pure spiritual milk so that you will grow into a full experience of salvation. Cry out for this nourishment,

I Peter 2:2 (AMP)

Like newborn babies you should crave (thirst for, earnestly desire) the pure (unadulterated) spiritual milk, that by it you may be nurtured and grow unto [completed] salvation,

Babies grow when they are fed, believers grow when they are fed. Romans 10:17 tells us when your spirit hears God's Word (faith comes and grows in your life; faith doesn't come from having heard sometime in the past but from a present hearing). Just like you may have had a wonderful meal last night for dinner, it may have been wonderfully satisfying, tasteful and nourishing, the only problem with it was it was yesterday's food and your body can't live off the memory of what you've eaten in the past. Our bodies have to be fed daily in order to grow and maintain health. So it is with your spirit and faith. The Word of God is 'faith food' for your spirit. Your faith will grow, become strong and maintain its strength when you daily feed it the Word of God.

The refining of your life's faith works like this, in whatever areas you sense the need to have a stronger, more developed faith, you must specifically search out and then study the promises of scripture concerning that area. For example: if you have a need for more of God's peace in your life, then find one or more scriptures that promise peace and build your faith by studying, memorizing and meditating (thinking) on them until peace comes. This same pattern works for any other area of life. For example, faith for healing comes by 'hearing' the promises of scripture concerning healing. Our faith can increase in any area of our life through hearing the promises of God's Word for that certain area.

THE RENEWING OF OUR MINDS

Romans 12:1-2 (NKJV)

I beseech you therefore, brethren, by the mercies of God, that you present your bodies a living sacrifice, holy, acceptable to God, which is your reasonable service. And do not be conformed to this world, but be transformed by the renewing of your mind, that you may prove what is that good and acceptable and perfect will of God.

Romans 12:1-2 (MSG)

So here's what I want you to do, God helping you: Take your everyday, ordinary life—your sleeping, eating, going-to-work, and walking-around life—and place it before God as an offering. Embracing what God does for you is the best thing you can do for him. Don't become so well-adjusted to your culture that you fit into it without even thinking. Instead, fix your attention on God. You'll be changed from the inside out. Readily recognize what he wants from you, and quickly respond to it. Unlike the culture around you, always dragging you down to its level of immaturity, God brings the best out of you, develops well-formed maturity in you.

Romans 12:1-2 (NLT)

And so, dear brothers and sisters, I plead with you to give your bodies to God because of all he has done for you. Let them be a living and holy sacrifice—the kind he will find acceptable. This is truly the way to worship him. Don't copy the behavior and customs of this world, but let God transform you into a new person by changing the way you think. Then you will learn to know God's will for you, which is good and pleasing and perfect.

Romans 12:1-2 (AMP)

I APPEAL to you therefore, brethren, and beg of you in view of [all] the mercies of God, to make a decisive dedication of your bodies [presenting all your members and faculties] as a living sacrifice, holy (devoted, consecrated) and well pleasing to God, which is your reasonable (rational, intelligent) service and spiritual worship. Do not be conformed to this world (this age), [fashioned after and adapted to its external, superficial customs], but be transformed (changed) by the [entire] renewal of your mind [by its new ideals and its new attitude], so that you may prove [for yourselves] what is the good and acceptable and perfect will of God, even the thing which is good and acceptable and perfect [in His sight for you].

"Let God transform you into a new person by changing the way you think." "Be changed from the inside out." "Be transformed by the renewing of your mind." Each of these translations of the Scriptures vividly reveals to us two important truths:

1. God wants to change our lives in every area.

2. Change only happens in our lives when real and lasting change occurs in our thoughts.

We experience this dynamic when we purposely introduce the Word of God into our thought life through the hearing, reading, studying, memorization and meditation of Scripture. After we have made the quality decision that God's Word is the final authority over all our lives, we then surrender to the truth of His word and with discipline, determination and patience, we renew our minds with His word.

Colossians 3:2(NKJV)
Set your mind on things above, not on things on the earth.

Colossians 3:2 (MSG)
Don't shuffle along, eyes to the ground, absorbed with the things right in front of you. Look up, and be alert to what is going on around Christ—that's where the action is. See things from his perspective.

Colossians 3:2 (NLT)
Think about the things of heaven, not the things of earth.

Colossians 3:9-16 (NKJV)
Do not lie to one another, since you have put off the old man with his deeds, and have put on the new man who is renewed in knowledge according to the image of Him who created him, where there is neither Greek nor Jew, circumcised nor uncircumcised, barbarian, Scythian, slave nor free, but Christ is all and in all. Therefore, as the elect of God, holy and beloved, put on tender mercies, kindness, humility, meekness, longsuffering; bearing with one another, and forgiving one another, if anyone has a complaint against another; even as Christ forgave you, so you also must do. But above all these things put on love, which is the bond of perfection. And let the peace of God rule in your hearts, to which also you were called in one body; and be thankful. Let the word of Christ dwell in you richly in all wisdom, teaching and admonishing one another in psalms and hymns and spiritual songs, singing with grace in your hearts to the Lord.

We continue to 'put on' and 'dress ourselves' in the newness of Christ by knowing, believing and meditating on the Scriptures. This is where our level of participation in the process determines the quality of the result.

Here's what Jesus said about His word and our hearts:

Matthew 13:3-9 (NKJV)

Then He spoke many things to them in parables, saying: "Behold, a sower went out to sow. And as he sowed, some seed fell by the wayside; and the birds came and devoured them. Some fell on stony places, where they did not have much earth; and they immediately sprang up because they had no depth of earth. But when the sun was up they were scorched, and because they had no root they withered away. And some fell among thorns, and the thorns sprang up and choked them. But others fell on good ground and yielded a crop: some a hundredfold, some sixty, some thirty. He who has ears to hear, let him hear!"

Matthew 13:3-9 (MSG)

"What do you make of this? A farmer planted seed. As he scattered the seed, some of it fell on the road, and birds ate it. Some fell in the gravel; it sprouted quickly but didn't put down roots, so when the sun came up it withered just as quickly. Some fell in the weeds; as it came up, it was strangled by the weeds. Some fell on good earth, and produced a harvest beyond his wildest dreams.
"Are you listening to this? Really listening?"

Matthew 13:18-23 (NKJV)

"Therefore hear the parable of the sower: When anyone hears the word of the kingdom, and does not understand it, then the wicked one comes and snatches away what was sown in his heart. This is he who received seed by the wayside. But he who received the seed on stony places, this is he who hears the word and immediately receives it with joy; yet he has no root in himself, but endures only for a while. For when tribulation or persecution arises because of the word, immediately he stumbles. Now he who received seed among the thorns is he who hears the word, and the cares of this world and the deceitfulness of riches choke the word, and he becomes unfruitful. But he who received seed on the good ground is he who hears the word and understands it, who indeed bears fruit and produces: some a hundredfold, some sixty, some thirty."

Matthew 13:18-23(MSG)

"Study this story of the farmer planting seed. When anyone hears news of the kingdom and doesn't take it in, it just remains on the surface, and so the Evil One comes along and plucks it right out of that person's heart. This is the seed the farmer scatters on the road.

"The seed cast in the gravel—this is the person who hears and instantly responds with enthusiasm. But there is no soil of character, and so when the emotions wear off and some difficulty arrives, there is nothing to show for it.

"The seed cast in the weeds is the person who hears the kingdom news, but weeds of worry and illusions about getting more and wanting everything under the sun strangle what was heard, and nothing comes of it.

"The seed cast on good earth is the person who hears and takes in the News, and then produces a harvest beyond his wildest dreams."

-the seed is the 'word of the kingdom'
-the soil is the human heart
-the birds represent Satan who wants to steal God's Word from your life. Don't let him! Ask for and cultivate an open and understanding heart.
-stony places are hearts that are shallow so that roots can't go deep. When pressure comes the crop fails under the heart, because of its lack of roots.
-the thorns are hearts that are living with too much worldly influence to ultimately be fruitful believers. The 'cares of the world' divert enough energy to steal real fruitfulness (covetousness, love of money)
-the good ground is the heart that hears the Word and understands it (always pray for the

Holy Spirit to give you revelation and understanding when you're reading or hearing God's Word. That's a prayer He will always answer!) To be good ground is the goal for every believer. Let's remove the stones, pull the weeds and plow the hard ground of our hearts so that the seed of the Word produces the harvest of His kingdom!

SUMMATION

-There are 66 books in the Bible
-There are two testaments, Old and New

-The New is in the Old concealed

-The Old is in the New revealed

-The New is in the Old enfolded

-The Old is in the New unfolded

-The New is in the Old explained

-The Old is in the New contained

CHAPTER 7
QUESTIONS AND ANSWERS

1. At the core and foundation of the church faith is the _____ _____ that the Bible is the _____ ___ _____.

2. The Bible does not represent the greatest and highest expressions of human intellectual enlightenment or consciousness, but _____ _____ the entirety of the Bible is _____ _____ _____ to us.

3. Men wrote the Scriptures as they were _____ ____ ____ _____ _____.

4. Everything we are to learn about God in this lifetime can only be safely and truthfully discovered through the _____ ____ _____ ____ ____ which in themselves are the _____ _____ ____ _____ ____ _____.

5. _____ means that in the original manuscripts of the books of the Bible there was no _____ ____ _____.

6. Inerrancy means that what we now read in our Bibles is _____ and _____ what God revealed by _____ _____ to themselves in the Scriptures.

7. _____ means the Bible is completely unfailing in its _____ and _____.

8. The Bible is the _____ _____ _____ ___ _____ Word of God.

9. When it is properly _____ _____ and _____ the seed of His word always _____ ____ _____ it has declared.

10. The seed (Word of God) is always perfect, the _____ (_____ _____) is when we must learn to _____ ____ _____ _____ to grow the seed.

11. The Bible will _____ to the degree of your _____ and _____ of it.

12. Hosea 4:6 says, "My people _____ _____ for a _____ _____ _____.

13. Jesus defines His true disciples as those who _____ ____ ____ _____.

14. It is only the _____ _____ _____ _____ that has the power to set us free.

15. The fool that _____ _____ or ____ ____ to our spirit is ____ _____ ____ _____.

16. In Matthew 4:4 Jesus said, "Man shall not live by _____ _____ but by _____ _____ _____.

17. Faith doesn't come from _____ _____ sometime in the past but from a _____ _____.

18. Your faith will _____ become _____ or _____ _____ when you daily _____ it the _____ ____ _____.

19. Real and lasting _____ only happens in our lives when real and lasting _____ occurs in our _____.

20. The New is in the Old _____

21. The Old is in the New _____

22. The New is in the Old _____

23. The Old is in the New_____

24. The New is in the Old _____

25. The Old is in the New _____

8 PRAYER

PRAYER: FACE TO FACE WITH GOD

The God that's redeemed us by the blood of His Son Jesus Christ longs for an intimate relationship, friendship and fellowship with us.

The way we engage and encounter God, person to person, is through prayer. Our God is alive. He is a real person. He is our loving heavenly Father and prayer is the way we spend time with Him, give Him our burdens and needs, and listen to His voice. (His voice can sometimes be heard by a 'still, small voice' in our hearts. Sometimes His voice is heard when He directs us to a passage of Scripture that He wishes to speak to us from). In prayer we allow Him the opportunity to minister His love, grace and kingdom into our lives. Prayer for us as believers is not an empty religious gesture or a demanded obligation and responsibility that we are to 'pay' Him as our 'duty.' Prayer is our lives greatest privilege and honor! The God of the universe opens His heart and hands to us with the invitation of unconditional access to Him anytime we choose! The rewards and benefits of prayer are powerful and plentiful to our lives.

Prayer changes things and shapes history. Prayer is the avenue by which God, in the fullness of His attributes and ability, becomes active in human affairs. Prayer is powerful because our God is powerful and it is through prayer His power and grace is released to mankind. Jesus teaches about prayer:

Luke 11:1 (NKJV)
Now it came to pass, as He was praying in a certain place, when He ceased, that one of His disciples said to Him, "Lord, teach us to pray, as John also taught his disciples."

Matthew 6:5-15 (NKJV)
"And when you pray, you shall not be like the hypocrites. For they love to pray standing in the synagogues and on the corners of the streets, that they may be seen by men. Assuredly, I say to you, they have their reward. But you, when you pray, go into your room, and when you have shut your door, pray to your Father who is in the secret place; and your Father who sees in secret will reward you openly. And when you pray, do not use vain repetitions as the heathen do. For they think that they will be heard for their many words.

"Therefore do not be like them. For your Father knows the things you have need of before you ask Him. In this manner, therefore, pray: Our Father in heaven, hallowed be Your name.

Your kingdom come. Your will be done on earth as it is in heaven.

Give us this day our daily bread.

And forgive us our debts, as we forgive our debtors.

And do not lead us into temptation, but deliver us from the evil one. For Yours is the kingdom and the power and the glory forever. Amen.

"For if you forgive men their trespasses, your heavenly Father will also forgive you. But if you do not forgive men their trespasses, neither will your Father forgive your trespasses."

Matthew 6:5-8, 14-15 (NKJV)
"And when you pray, you shall not be like the hypocrites. For they love to pray standing in the synagogues and on the corners of the streets, that they may be seen by men. Assuredly, I say to you, they have their reward. But you, when you pray, go into your room, and when you have shut your door, pray to your Father who is in the secret place; and your Father who sees in secret will reward you openly. And

when you pray, do not use vain repetitions as the heathen do. For they think that they will be heard for their many words.

"Therefore do not be like them. For your Father knows the things you have need of before you ask Him.

"For if you forgive men their trespasses, your heavenly Father will also forgive you. But if you do not forgive men their trespasses, neither will your Father forgive your trespasses."

Jesus said that prayer was a personal and intimate act of surrender, love and petition between men and God. He warned against meaningless recital and repetition in our prayer. The Greek word for prayer is proseuche – which is a compound word made up of 'pros' and 'euche'. The word pros is a preposition that means towards and it denotes a sense of closeness. One scholar says the word pros is used to portray the intimate relationship that exists between the members of the Godhead. (We believe in One God represented in three persons: Father, Son and Holy Spirit. We call this the "Trinity" because although there are three Persons, they are perfectly united as one). "The Word was God." In the beginning, the Word was "face to face with God." Pros means close, up front, intimate contact with someone else.

The second part of the Greek word used for prayer, proseuche, is euche. It is an old Greek word that describes a prayer, wish, desire or vow. It was originally used to depict a person who made some kind of vow to God because of some need or desire in his or her life. This individual would vow to give God something of great value in exchange for a favorable answer to prayer.

In Greek culture, before prayer was verbalized and offered to a 'god,' a commemorative altar was set up and thanksgiving was offered on the altar. Such offerings of praise and thanksgiving were called 'votive offerings.' The person would promise that once his prayer had been answered, he would be back to give additional thanksgiving to his 'god.' Those votive offerings of praise and worship were elaborate and well-planned. Giving thanks to a deity was a significant event, so it was done in a serious and grandiose manner to outwardly demonstrate a thankful heart.

This is the most used word in the New Testament for prayer. Because most readers of Paul's epistles were Greek in origin, this word painted a vivid word picture to them of prayer.

It portrayed an individual who desired to see his prayer answered so desperately that he was willing to surrender everything he owned in exchange for answered prayer. Clearly this demonstrates an altar of sacrifice and consecration in prayer whereby a believer's life is yielded entirely to God. The idea of proseuche is "come face to face with God and surrender your life in exchange for answered prayer." Maintain an attitude of consecration as an ongoing part of your life and be sure to give Him thanks for moving on your behalf.

Jesus said for us to come worshipfully to God in prayer, acknowledging the greatness of God and His wonderful attributes. As Jesus taught us about who God is, over 150 times in the gospels Jesus addressed God as "Father" and Jesus brings us into His family by His blood and tells us to talk to God as our Father also.

"Holy is Your name." Holiness is an attribute of God. We are not to stop with this one sentence, but the 'Lord's prayer' is in reality an outline for prayer, not a formula we are to mindlessly repeat in prayer. Praising and worshipping is the proper practice for us to come and go from the King's presence in prayer.

Jesus then introduced the theme of what prayer is "Your kingdom come! Your will be done on earth as it is in heaven."

The tense and mood of the structure of these in the Greek is declarative. Literally, it reads, "Come Your kingdom! Come your will!" In prayer we are to boldly, confidently and expectantly declare the Kingdom and will of God into our lives and world. Prayer brings heaven to earth. Prayer releases God's will (as declared in His word) to be done "on earth as it is in heaven." Prayer makes the impossible possible. Please understand this, God does nothing in the earth without being asked, invited and released to by someone's prayer. When He created the world, He gave His children, Adam and Eve, authority and dominion over His creation. Through sin man lost most of his dominion and authority, but in the redemption that Jesus brings to us in the kingdom of God, the restoration of God's original creative intent given to Adam is now restored through the last Adam, Jesus Christ. In the Kingdom of God we have been repaired in authority so that our prayers are the powerful declaration of kingdom dominion in the earth.

Jesus said to pray "Give us this day our daily bread." We are to confidently ask for the material needs of our lives to be met in prayer. Our 'daily bread' includes the many areas of need and provision that we are invited to ask God's provision for. Jesus then said to both ask for and express forgiveness; as we 'confess' our sins He is 'faithful and just' to forgive all our sins. By connecting our freely given and received forgiveness from God, we then need to be forgiving towards others.

When we stop forgiving people, we break away from God's grace, and we disqualify our prayers through unforgiveness. Because we are forgiven of everything by God, He reasonably expects us to be forgiving towards people. We are to forgive everyone of everything all the time. Forgiveness towards others keeps the "heavens open" over our lives so our prayers can be heard and answered by God.

Jesus said to pray, "Lead us not into temptation, but deliver us from the evil one."

In prayer we are strengthened to be able to overcome the assaults of the enemy against our lives.

> James 4:7
> Therefore submit to God. Resist the devil and he will flee from you.

When we 'submit to God' through prayer, He equips us to be able to 'resist the devil.' The importance of prayer to overcome the enemy is shown in Ephesians 6:10-18(NKJV):

> Finally, my brethren, be strong in the Lord and in the power of His might. Put on the whole armor of God, that you may be able to stand against the wiles of the devil. For we do not wrestle against flesh and blood, but against principalities, against powers, against the rulers of the darkness of this age, against spiritual hosts of wickedness in the heavenly places. Therefore take up the whole armor of God,

that you may be able to withstand in the evil day, and having done all, to stand.

Stand therefore, having girded your waist with truth, having put on the breastplate of righteousness, and having shod your feet with the preparation of the gospel of peace; above all, taking the shield of faith with which you will be able to quench all the fiery darts of the wicked one. And take the helmet of salvation, and the sword of the Spirit, which is the word of God; praying always with all prayer and supplication in the Spirit, being watchful to this end with all perseverance and supplication for all the saints

Ephesians 6:10-18 (MSG)

And that about wraps it up. God is strong, and he wants you strong. So take everything the Master has set out for you, well-made weapons of the best materials. And put them to use so you will be able to stand up to everything the Devil throws your way. This is no afternoon athletic contest that we'll walk away from and forget about in a couple of hours. This is for keeps, a life-or-death fight to the finish against the Devil and all his angels.

Be prepared. You're up against far more than you can handle on your own. Take all the help you can get, every weapon God has issued, so that when it's all over but the shouting you'll still be on your feet. Truth, righteousness, peace, faith, and salvation are more than words. Learn how to apply them. You'll need them throughout your life. God's Word is an indispensable weapon. In the same way, prayer is essential in this ongoing warfare. Pray hard and long. Pray for your brothers and sisters. Keep your eyes open. Keep each other's spirits up so that no one falls behind or drops out.

The Greek word for 'whole armor' is panoplia – it describes the full battle and display armor of the most heavily armed infantry in the Roman army. Each piece of this armor represents an attitude and behavior we are to incorporate in prayer.

I. Gird your waist with truth

An essential element to 'becoming strong' in the Lord is pictured here – Integrity.

I John 1:9-10 (NKJV)

If we confess our sins, He is faithful and just to forgive us our sins and to cleanse us from all unrighteousness. If we say that we have not sinned, we make Him a liar, and His word is not in us.

Matthew 5:8 (NKJV)
Blessed are the pure in heart, for they shall see God.

Psalm 66:18 (NKJV)
If I regard iniquity in my heart, the Lord will not hear.

The first step in putting on our prayer armor is to practice personal integrity by being transparent and completely honest with God. Integrity produces spiritual power.

II. Breastplate of Righteousness

We put on our breastplate by acknowledging and claiming the great gift of 'right standing' with God we've been given by the blood of Jesus Christ.

II Corinthians 5:21 (NKJV)
For He made Him who knew no sin to be sin for us, that we might become the righteousness of God in Him.

Romans 5:17 (NKJV)
For if by the one man's offense death reigned through the one, much more those who receive abundance of grace and of the gift of righteousness will reign in life through the One, Jesus Christ.)

Isaiah 61:10 (NKJV)
I will greatly rejoice in the LORD, my soul shall be joyful in my God; for He has clothed me with the garments of salvation, He has covered me with the robe of righteousness, as a bridegroom decks himself with ornaments, and as a bride adorns herself with her jewels.

Righteousness is a gift. We can't earn it and don't deserve it, but are to welcome it with gratefulness and praise to God. As we more and more identify with our new nature of righteousness, we'll begin to more and more live it out by a more Christ-like life.

III. Feet Shod with the Gospel of Peace

Peace is a spiritual weapon. Note this about the Roman soldier's shoes:

> They extended from the knee to the foot. The part that covered the knees to the feet was called "greaves" – made of metal and wrapped around the calves. The shoe was made of heavy pieces of leather or of metal, tied together with leather straps that were intermingled with bits of metal. They were vicious weapons. The bottom of the shoes were made with heavy leather and pieces of metal – affixed with sharp, dangerous spikes. Two sharply pointed spikes extended beyond the front of each shoe. The soldier would stomp his shoe down so that spikes on the bottom would go into the ground allowing him to 'stand' against his adversary, because his feet were planted. In battle the soldier would also use his shoes as vicious weapons by kicking at his combat adversary. The long spikes at the front of his shoe were sharp and deadly weapons in battle.

God's peace is a spiritual weapon we are to use to plant our lives immoveable on the promise of God and to 'kick at' the enemy's assault of fear when it comes.

Philippians 4:6-7 (NKJV)
Be anxious for nothing, but in everything by prayer and supplication, with thanksgiving, let your requests be made known to God; and the peace of God, which surpasses all understanding, will guard your hearts and minds through Christ Jesus.

Colossians 3:15 (NKJV)
And let the peace of God rule in your hearts, to which also you were called in one body; and be thankful.

John 14:27 (NKJV)
Peace I leave with you, My peace I give to you; not as the world gives do I give to you. Let not your heart be troubled, neither let it be afraid.

Psalm 29:11 (NKJV)

The LORD will give strength to His people; the LORD will bless His people with peace.

Isaiah 26:3 (NKJV)

You will keep him in perfect peace, whose mind is stayed on You, because he trusts in You.

IV. The Shield of Faith

A Roman soldier's shield was composed of multiple layers, usually six, of thick animal hide that had been tanned. This process made the shield extremely tough and exceptionally durable.

The Roman soldier's shield required daily maintenance in order to keep up its excellent condition. Early morning, when he awoke, the soldier would take a piece of cloth completely saturated with oil. Then he would begin to rub the oil into the leather portion of the shield to keep it soft, supple and pliable.

If not properly maintained, the leather would harden and crack when put under pressure and finally fall into pieces. It could easily cost a soldier his very life if his shield was not properly maintained.

Before the battle the soldier would soak his shield in water until it was completely saturated. It was then able to quench every fiery arrow of the enemy.

Our faith is an irreplaceable part of our armor. Just as it was the individual soldier's personal responsibility to maintain the good condition of his shield, it is our responsibility, as believers, to do the 'daily maintenance' required for our faith to remain strong.

Romans 10:17 (NKJV)
So then faith comes by hearing, and hearing by the Word of God.

When we feed our faith the 'daily bread' of God's Word it will grow strong.

I John 5:4 (NKJV)

For whatever is born of God overcomes the world. And this is the victory that has overcome the world—our faith.

Jude 1:20 (NKJV)

But you, beloved, building yourselves up on your most holy faith, praying in the Holy Spirit...

V. The Helmet of Salvation

The Roman soldier's helmet was a fascinating and flamboyant piece of armor, very ornate and intricate.

It was highly decorated with all kinds of engravings and etchings. The helmet looked more like a beautiful piece of artwork than a simple piece of metal formed to fit the head of a soldier.

It was not uncommon for a Roman soldier's helmet to be decorated with depictions of pastoral farm scenes, complete with all kinds of animals (horses, elephants, etc).
The helmet was made of bronze and was equipped with pieces of armor that were specifically designed to protect the cheeks and jaws.

It was extremely heavy, therefore the interior was lined with sponge in order to soften its weight on the soldier's head.

This piece of armor was so strong, so massive, and so heavy that nothing could pierce it, not even a hammer or battle axe.

Romans 12:2 (NKJV)

And do not be conformed to this world, but be transformed by the renewing of your mind, that you may prove what is that good and acceptable and perfect will of God.

Our minds are to be protected by the helmet of salvation, the renewed mind that we can put on as believers.

VI. The Sword of the Spirit – The Word of God

The Greek word used to describe the Roman soldier's 'two-edged' sword is distomos, which literally means "two mouthed." Our prayers become the most effective and powerful they can be when we incorporate God's Word into them. The 'two-mouthed' sword is a picture of God's Word coming to us in revelation making one side of the two-edged (two-mouthed) sword. When we then speak His word out loud in our prayers, the other half of the sword is then formed to make it the great weapon over the enemy God's given to us.

Hebrews 4:12 (NKJV)
For the word of God is living and powerful, and sharper than any two-edged sword, piercing even to the division of soul and spirit, and of joints and marrow, and is a discerner of the thoughts and intents of the heart.

Psalm 149:5-9 (NKJV)
Let the saints be joyful in glory; let them sing aloud on their beds.
Let the high praises of God be in their mouth, and a two-edged sword in their hand, to execute vengeance on the nations, and punishments on the peoples; to bind their kings with chains, and their nobles with fetters of iron; to execute on them the written judgment—This honor have all His saints. Praise the LORD!

Wearing the 'whole armor of God' we are then to "pray always with all prayer and supplication in the Spirit."

Prayer greatly benefits our life when we exchange our cares and burdens for God's peace and rest.

Philippians 4:6-7 (NKJV)
Be anxious for nothing, but in everything by prayer and supplication, with thanksgiving, let your requests be made known to God; and the peace of God, which surpasses all understanding, will guard your hearts and minds through Christ Jesus.

Philippians 4:6-7 (MSG)

Don't fret or worry. Instead of worrying, pray. Let petitions and praises shape your worries into prayers, letting God know your concerns. Before you know it, a sense of God's wholeness, everything coming together for good, will come and settle you down. It's wonderful what happens when Christ displaces worry at the center of your life.

I Peter 5:7 (NKJV)

...casting all your care upon Him, for He cares for you.

Here is a brief description of various kinds and types of prayer available to us.

1. The Prayer of Agreement – When two (or more) believers unite together in faith while asking God in prayer for something.

Matthew 18:19 (NKJV)

"Again I say to you that if two of you agree on earth concerning anything that they ask, it will be done for them by My Father in heaven.

Matthew 18:19 (MSG)

I mean this. When two of you get together on anything at all on earth and make a prayer of it, my Father in heaven goes into action.

2. The Prayer of Petition and Supplication – When we ask God in a specific request.

Philippians 4:6 (NKJV)

Be anxious for nothing, but in everything by prayer and supplication, with thanksgiving, let your requests be made known to God;

I Timothy 2:1 (NKJV)

Therefore I exhort first of all that supplications, prayers, intercessions, and giving of thanks be made for all men...

Supplication – Greek word deisis – petition for need to be met, a person who has some type of lack in his life and therefore pleads strongly for his need to be met, to earnestly appeal.

This word pictures a person in such great need that he feels compelled to push his pride out of the way so he can boldly, earnestly, strongly and passionately cry out for someone to help or assist him. Deisis (supplication) is a passionate, earnest, heartfelt, sincere prayer - a heartfelt request for God to answer a concrete, specific request.

> Psalm 34:17 (NKJV)
>
> The righteous cry out, and the LORD hears, and delivers them out of all their troubles.

3. The Prayer of Faith – Exercising bold authority, based on God's Word, to declare healing, deliverance and freedom in the name of Jesus.

> James 5:14-18 (NKJV)
>
> Is anyone among you sick? Let him call for the elders of the church, and let them pray over him, anointing him with oil in the name of the Lord. And the prayer of faith will save the sick, and the Lord will raise him up. And if he has committed sins, he will be forgiven. Confess your trespasses to one another, and pray for one another, that you may be healed. The effective, fervent prayer of a righteous man avails much. Elijah was a man with a nature like ours, and he prayed earnestly that it would not rain; and it did not rain on the land for three years and six months. And he prayed again, and the heaven gave rain, and the earth produced its fruit.

> Acts 3:6-7, 16 (NKJV)
>
> Then Peter said, "Silver and gold I do not have, but what I do have I give you: In the name of Jesus Christ of Nazareth, rise up and walk." And he took him by the right hand and lifted him up, and immediately his feet and ankle bones received strength.
>
> And His name, through faith in His name, has made this man strong, whom you see and know. Yes, the faith which comes through Him has given him this perfect soundness in the presence of you all.

Mark 16:17-18 (NKJV)

And these signs will follow those who believe: In My name they will cast out demons; they will speak with new tongues; they will take up serpents; and if they drink anything deadly, it will by no means hurt them; they will lay hands on the sick, and they will recover."

4. The Prayer of Binding and Loosing – When believers take authority in prayer to stop (bind) the enemy's works and activity and then release (loose) the will and kingdom of God.

Matthew 16:19 (NKJV)

And I will give you the keys of the kingdom of heaven, and whatever you bind on earth will be bound in heaven, and whatever you loose on earth will be loosed in heaven."

Matthew 16:19 (MSG)

"And that's not all. You will have complete and free access to God's kingdom, keys to open any and every door: no more barriers between heaven and earth, earth and heaven. A yes on earth is yes in heaven. A no on earth is no in heaven."

Matthew 16:19 (NLT)

And I will give you the keys of the Kingdom of Heaven. Whatever you forbid on earth will be forbidden in heaven, and whatever you permit on earth will be permitted in heaven."

Matthew 18:18 (NKJV)

"Assuredly, I say to you, whatever you bind on earth will be bound in heaven, and whatever you loose on earth will be loosed in heaven.

5. The Prayer of Consecration – When we surrender our lives in any aspect or decision to the will of God in prayer. This prayer is portrayed by Christ in:

Matthew 26:39 (NKJV)

He went a little farther and fell on His face, and prayed, saying, "O My Father, if it is possible, let this cup pass from Me; nevertheless, not as I will, but as You will."

Matthew 26:39 (NLT)

He went on a little farther and bowed with his face to the ground, praying, "My Father! If it is possible, let this cup of suffering be taken away from me. Yet I want your will to be done, not mine."

It is the place of surrendering our will and desires to God's will.

6. The Prayer of Intercession – When we take the place of others in prayer for their salvation, healing or needs.

I Timothy 2:1-2 (NKJV)

Therefore I exhort first of all that supplications, prayers, intercessions, and giving of thanks be made for all men, for kings and all who are in authority, that we may lead a quiet and peaceable life in all godliness and reverence.

The Holy Spirit is always searching for true intercessors who will cry out to God for others.

Ezekiel 22:30 (NKJV)

So I sought for a man among them who would make a wall, and stand in the gap before Me on behalf of the land, that I should not destroy it; but I found no one.

7. The Prayer in the Spirit – When we pray in our heavenly language, urged on by the leading of the Holy Spirit.

Romans 8:26-27 (NKJV)

Likewise the Spirit also helps in our weaknesses. For we do not know what we should pray for as we ought, but the Spirit Himself makes intercession for us with groanings which cannot be uttered. Now He who searches the hearts knows what the mind of the Spirit is, because He makes intercession for the saints according to the will of God.

Ephesians 6:18 (NKJV)
...praying always with all prayer and supplication in the Spirit, being watchful to this end with all perseverance and supplication for all the saints . . .

We are instructed in Scripture to lift our prayers to our heavenly Father in the name of Jesus.

John 15:16 (NKJV)
You did not choose Me, but I chose you and appointed you that you should go and bear fruit, and that your fruit should remain, that whatever you ask the Father in My name He may give you.

John 16:23-24 (NKJV)
"And in that day you will ask Me nothing. Most assuredly, I say to you, whatever you ask the Father in My name He will give you. Until now you have asked nothing in My name. Ask, and you will receive, that your joy may be full.

8. The Prayer of Thanksgiving – Praise and deep gratitude should always be a part of our dialogue of prayer with God. The Greek word for pray carries the idea of thanking being made before a request is made in prayer.

Philippians 4:6 (NKJV)
Be anxious for nothing, but in everything by prayer and supplication, with thanksgiving, let your requests be made known to God;

Notice "with thanksgiving" as being a part of the prayer life of believers.

I Thessalonians 5:16-18 (NKJV)
Rejoice always, pray without ceasing, in everything give thanks; for this is the will of God in Christ Jesus for you.

The Greek word for thanksgiving is eucharistos which means "an outpouring of grace and wonderful feelings that freely flow from the heart in response to someone or something. To be grateful, to express gratitude."

Luke 17:11-19 (NKJV)
Now it happened as He went to Jerusalem that He passed through the midst of Samaria and Galilee. Then as He entered a certain village, there met Him ten men who were lepers, who stood afar off. And they lifted up their voices and said, "Jesus, Master, have mercy on us!"

So when He saw them, He said to them, "Go, show yourselves to the priests." And so it was that as they went, they were cleansed.

And one of them, when he saw that he was healed, returned, and with a loud voice glorified God, and fell down on his face at His feet, giving Him thanks. And he was a Samaritan.

So Jesus answered and said, "Were there not ten cleansed? But where are the nine? Were there not any found who returned to give glory to God except this foreigner?" And He said to him, "Arise, go your way. Your faith has made you well."

Jesus asked, "Where are the nine?" He had healed ten lepers, but only one made the effort to come back to Jesus to express his deep gratitude and thanksgiving. What happened next is incredible. This singularly thankful man was given an even greater miracle, the full restoration of his body from the devastation that leprosy had brought him. All ten lepers were healed from their leprosy, but only one had a miraculous, creative miracle that manifested by fingers, toes and facial features being supernaturally restored! (Leprosy eats away the extremities, skin and organs of those who have it.) His thanksgiving allowed the healing work of Christ to continue until he was made completely whole.

CHAPTER 8
QUESTIONS AND ANSWERS

1. The God of the universe opens His heart and hands to us with the _____ ____ _____ _____ to Him anytime we choose.

2. Prayer _____ _____ and _____ _____.

3. Jesus said that prayer was _____ and _____ _____ of surrender, love and petition between _____ and _____.

4. As Jesus taught us about who God is, over 150 times in the gospels, He addresses God as _____.

5. In prayer we are to _____ _____ and _____ declare the _____ ____ _____ and _____ ____ _____ into our lives and world.

6. Prayer makes the impossible _____.

7. God does nothing in the earth without being _____, _____ and _____ to by someone's _____.

8. In battle, the Roman soldier would use his shoes as _____ _____ by kicking at his combat adversary.

9. God's peace is a _____ _____ we are to use to _____ ____ _____ immoveable on the promises of God and to _____ ____ the enemies assault of fear when it comes.

10. What is the prayer of agreement? _____

11. We are instructed in Scripture to lift our prayers to our _____ _____ in the name of _____.

12. The Greek word for prayer carries with it the idea of _____ being made _____ and _____ a request is made in prayer.

9 THE CHURCH

In people's minds, opinions and beliefs the word 'church' conjures up many different ideas. Whatever you've heard, experienced or have thought about 'church,' let's start from the beginning by examining what God's Word has to say about the church. If we base our understanding, beliefs and personal involvement concerning the church on God's Word, then we'll have the opportunity to experience the full promise of God's will and kingdom.

JESUS CHRIST IS THE CREATOR, FOUNDER AND BUILDER OF THE CHURCH!

Matthew 16:18 (KJV)

And I say also unto thee, That thou art Peter, and upon this rock I will build my church; and the gates of hell shall not prevail against it.

Matthew 16:18 (MSG)

And now I'm going to tell you who you are, really are. You are Peter, a rock. This is the rock on which I will put together my church, a church so expansive with energy that not even the gates of hell will be able to keep it out.

Matthew 16:18 (AMP)

And I tell you, you are Peter [Greek, Petros--a large piece of rock], and on this rock [Greek, petra—a huge rock like Gibraltar] I will build My church, and the gates of Hades (the powers of the infernal region) shall not overpower it [or be strong to its detriment or hold out against it].

The church is not man's idea or dream. It is God's idea and dream. Jesus said that He would "Build My church." The church belongs to Jesus and He is the One that builds it. The church has survived over 2,000 years of hostility, persecution, mens' attempts to control and reshape it, Satan's vicious attacks and the failure of some leaders and members in it. The church has survived, prospered and grown exponentially throughout the ages because God is the One building and blessing it. Now, when I say 'church,' let's define what that means according to the scriptures. Much of what we now call 'church' is far from any likeness to what the design of God revealed in the Scriptures says it should be. So if there's been a failure in following the biblical pattern and design for the church, there will always be an inferior product than what God intended man to experience. When we use mens' ideas as the replacement for God's Word, the result may be called "church," but it's not the same as what God calls "the church."

The word Christ used for 'church' is the Greek word ecclesia which means "an assembly of citizens, called out ones, a body of free citizens called together by a herald." The church in the earth today is comprised of every born again believer in every community, country and continent in the world. This is what is called the 'church universal.' Every member of God's family (those who have received the free gift of salvation through Jesus Christ have been adopted in God's family) around the world is also a part of His church. Now you can legitimately and legally belong to something but not fully participate in it. (Like owning a membership to the fitness center, but never showing up to work out!) Every believer is not only a member of God's universal church, they are to then participate in the life of a Christ-honoring, Bible believing and teaching, Spirit empowered local church.

THE 'WINESKIN' (BIBLICAL STRUCTURE) OF THE CHURCH

The Bible gives us specific instruction into what are the ingredients necessary in the 'wineskin' or biblical structure of the church.

Ephesians 4:11-16 (NKJV)

And He Himself gave some to be apostles, some prophets, some evangelists, and some pastors and teachers, for the equipping of the saints for the work of ministry, for the edifying of the body of Christ, till we all come to the unity of the faith and of the knowledge of the Son of God, to a perfect man, to the measure of the stature of the fullness of Christ; that we should no longer be children, tossed to and fro and carried about with every wind of doctrine, by the trickery of men, in the cunning craftiness of deceitful plotting, but, speaking the truth in love, may grow up in all things into Him who is the head—Christ— from whom the whole body, joined and knit together by what every joint supplies, according to the effective working by which every part does its share, causes growth of the body for the edifying of itself in love.

Ephesians 4:11-16 (MSG)

He handed out gifts of apostle, prophet, evangelist, and pastor-teacher to train Christ's followers in skilled servant work, working within Christ's body, the church, until we're all moving rhythmically and easily with each other, efficient and graceful in response to God's Son, fully mature adults, fully developed within and without, fully alive like Christ.

No prolonged infancies among us, please. We'll not tolerate babes in the woods, small children who are an easy mark for impostors. God wants us to grow up, to know the whole truth and tell it in love—like Christ in everything. We take our lead from Christ, who is the source of everything we do. He keeps us in step with each other. His very breath and blood flow through us, nourishing us so that we will grow up healthy in God, robust in love

Ephesians 4:11-16 (NLT)

Now these are the gifts Christ gave to the church: the apostles, the prophets, the evangelists, and the pastors and teachers. Their responsibility is to equip God's people to do his work and build up the church, the body of Christ. This will continue until we all come to such unity in our faith and knowledge of God's Son that we will be mature in the Lord, measuring up to the full and complete standard of Christ.

Then we will no longer be immature like children. We won't be tossed and blown about by every wind of new teaching. We will not be influenced when people try to trick us with lies so clever they sound like the truth. Instead, we will speak the truth in love, growing in every way more and more like Christ, who is the head of his body, the church. He makes the whole body fit together perfectly. As each part does its own special work, it helps the other parts grow, so that the whole body is healthy and growing and full of love.

When Christ ascended in absolute victory into heaven after vanquishing sin, Satan and sickness, He sent to mankind through the Holy Spirit five unique and anointed office gifts. Those five office gifts of His grace are apostles, prophets, evangelists, pastors and teachers. He divided the perfectly complete anointing of His own Person and grace into these five different office gifts, so that together they form a complete and comprehensive expression of the ministry of Christ in the church. At no time has He or any scripture in the Bible declared that these spiritual gifts given to mankind are no longer the essential and irreplaceable elements necessary in the construction of the church. Any religious tradition, denomination or modern theology that has discarded the biblical pattern of the church for man's concepts and designs is in error. It is simply wrong to change into man's image what is to be built in likeness to the divinely declared design of God.

When the church lacks one or more of these five office gifts, it will always have an incomplete and imperfect expression of the grace of Christ in equipping believers. These five gifts are like 'coaches' that are called to train their teams for victory in their sport.

FIVE-FOLD MINISTRY GIFTS

I. Apostles – Are highest in rank and responsibility.

They are mature, spiritual fathers who have grace to pioneer churches, mature believers, and raise up and disciple leaders.

> I Corinthians 12:28 (NKJV)
> And God has appointed these in the church: first apostles, second prophets, third teachers, after that miracles, then gifts of healings, helps, administrations, varieties of tongues.

> Ephesians 2:20 (NKJV)
> ...having been built on the foundation of the apostles and prophets, Jesus Christ Himself being the chief cornerstone,

> Ephesians 3:5 (NKJV)
> ...which in other ages was not made known to the sons of men, as it has now been revealed by the Spirit to His holy apostles and prophets:

As with all five offices, these spiritual fathers are not called to be self-serving dictators, but instead, self-sacrificing servants.

> I Peter 5:1-4 (NKJV)
> The elders who are among you I exhort, I who am a fellow elder and a witness of the sufferings of Christ, and also a partaker of the glory that will be revealed: Shepherd the flock of God which is among you, serving as overseers, not by compulsion but willingly, not for dishonest gain but eagerly; nor as being lords over those entrusted to you, but being examples to the flock; and when the Chief Shepherd appears, you will receive the crown of glory that does not fade away.

Apostles are to operate in the Holy Spirit gifts and see the miraculous.

> II Corinthians 12:12 (NKJV)
> Truly the signs of an apostle were accomplished among you with all perseverance, in signs and wonders and mighty deeds.

Apostles engage in the overseeing of churches and ministries, serving as spiritual coverings, mentors and guides.

All five of these are assigned and anointed "to equip the church to do the work of ministry." The grace of God expressed through their teaching, preaching and ministering brings maturity and growth to the members of the church so that they can then be effective in their ministry to others in the body of Christ. Every believer is called to minister. The purpose of these five gifts is to prepare, furnish and equip people for their place of ministry in the body of Christ.

II. Prophets – Are anointed by the Holy Spirit to reveal God's Word, will, calling and destiny to believers.

They are gifted in prophecy, seeing visions and dreams. Many times they are given supernatural insight concerning the future.

Ephesians 2:20 (NKJV)
. . . having been built on the foundation of the apostles and prophets, Jesus Christ Himself being the chief cornerstone,

Acts 11:27-30 (NKJV)
And in these days prophets came from Jerusalem to Antioch. Then one of them, named Agabus, stood up and showed by the Spirit that there was going to be a great famine throughout all the world, which also happened in the days of Claudius Caesar. Then the disciples, each according to his ability, determined to send relief to the brethren dwelling in Judea. This they also did, and sent it to the elders by the hands of Barnabas and Saul.

Deuteronomy 18:20-22 (NKJV)
But the prophet who presumes to speak a word in My name, which I have not commanded him to speak, or who speaks in the name of other gods, that prophet shall die.' And if you say in your heart, 'How shall we know the word which the LORD has not spoken?'— when a prophet speaks in the name of the LORD, if the thing does not happen or come to pass, that is the thing which the LORD has not

spoken; the prophet has spoken it presumptuously; you shall not be afraid of him.

Throughout the Bible, prophets were used of God to teach, preach, and demonstrate signs, wonders and miracles. Although every believer can move in the gift of prophecy, every person who prophesies is not a prophet. Prophets work with Apostles as the two 'foundational' gifts of the church. Note that all of God's people are called to participate in the life of a local church - that means those who have office gifts also. We are all called, no matter our status, experience or achievement, to submit our lives to the spiritual oversight of these five office gifts. Everyone needs to be 'pastored' in this sense – including those in the ministry.

III. Evangelists – Are anointed by the Holy Spirit in the winning of souls to Christ and in the equipping of believers to do the same.

II Timothy 4:5 (NKJV)

But you be watchful in all things, endure afflictions, do the work of an evangelist, fulfill your ministry.

Acts 21:8 (NKJV)

On the next day we who were Paul's companions departed and came to Caesarea, and entered the house of Philip the evangelist, who was one of the seven, and stayed with him.

IV. Pastors – Are anointed by the Holy Spirit to care, feed and lead the local church. Pastors are essential to the discipleship, growth and maturity of all believers.

I Peter 5:1-3 (NKJV)

The elders who are among you I exhort, I who am a fellow elder and a witness of the sufferings of Christ, and also a partaker of the glory that will be revealed: Shepherd the flock of God which is among you, serving as overseers, not by compulsion but willingly, not for dishonest gain but eagerly; nor as being lords over those entrusted to you, but being examples to the flock;

V. Teachers – Are anointed to receive clear revelation of the truths of God's Word and then systematically teach those principles to the church.

I Corinthians 12:28 (NKJV)

And God has appointed these in the church: first apostles, second prophets, third teachers, after that miracles, then gifts of healings, helps, administrations, varieties of tongues.

II Timothy 2:2, 24 (NKJV)

And the things that you have heard from me among many witnesses, commit these to faithful men who will be able to teach others also. And a servant of the Lord must not quarrel but be gentle to all, able to teach, patient...

In the ancient Greece and Roman empires, the concept of the ecclesia (church) was practiced this way. When the empire would take new territory in the world, they would choose out of that territory a group of handpicked regional leaders, whom they would then bring back to their governmental headquarters. Once they arrived at the seat of power in that kingdom, these 'called out' ones were given the assignment to study and learn the customs of the culture and the mind and methods of the king. They were granted unusual access into the government in order to see and learn everything they could about this new kingdom and king. Upon completion of this prolonged season of learning, after they were judged 'ready' by those overseeing their training, they were then sent back to the various regions of the world where they originally came from as official ambassadors and representatives of the new kingdom. This paints a beautiful picture of the purpose of the church in the world. The church is to teach, train and prepare God's people in the ways and principles of God's kingdom and then to release them back to the world from which they were called out of as ambassadors of Christ and His heavenly kingdom. The rulers of the ancient empires of Rome and Greece knew that once the ecclesia, these hand-selected chosen ones, had learned the mind of Caesar and the principles by which he governed his kingdom, they would then be successful at accurately representing the kingdom in its far away territories. The same is true for the purpose of the church, to train God's people to accurately represent Christ and His kingdom to all the world. That's why we'll never not need the church, because we'll never not need to be further developed in our representation of Christ (Christlikeness) and His glorious kingdom.

WHAT DID CHRIST REALLY MEAN WHEN HE SAID "MANY ARE CALLED, BUT FEW ARE CHOSEN?"

Matthew 22:14 (NKJV)
"For many are called, but few are chosen."

Matthew 22:14 (MSG)
"That's what I mean when I say, 'Many get invited; only a few make it.'"

Matthew 22:14 (AMP)
For many are called (invited and summoned), but few are chosen.

This statement of Christ was a direct adaptation of the motto and mission of the Roman army. Everyone who heard Christ preach lived under the control of the Roman Empire and its powerful army. When He used this phrase, "Many are called, but few are chosen" they who heard Him understood exactly what He meant.

In the Roman Empire the highest, most prestigious and honored vocation for a man was to be a soldier in the Roman army. Every man's childhood dream was to someday be a part of that most powerful group. Boys would begin training in early childhood to become soldiers in the Roman army. In each spring every man of age from every province of the entire Roman Empire was invited ('called') to come to the city of Rome where there was the great Roman army training grounds called Campus Martius. The great fields of this massive military training base would fill up with tens of thousands of men who were being trained in every activity involved in soldiering. On these fields and also sitting watchfully in the grandstands surrounding them were hundreds of experienced military leaders. These leaders were engaged in both training potential warriors and then carefully observing those who they deemed ready for immediate military service.

When a man was deemed ready, a leader would meet with him to congratulate him for being "chosen." Being 'chosen' never happened by chance. When a man was chosen it was solely because he had proven himself on the training grounds of Campus Martius as being fully prepared for battle. He had learned and incorporated his training into his own behavior and skills. Every year many more soldiers were not chosen than were chosen. Those that the leaders judged not quite ready for military employment were not condemned, belittled or mocked. Instead they were graciously honored for their passion and effort and invited back to next year's tryouts ('calling'). Those that heard Christ speak "Many are called, but few are chosen" understood what I just shared with you. The church that Jesus is building is the kingdom of God's Campus Martius in the earth. It is the place where every single believer in Christ is 'called' to participate in.

What we've experienced and understood the church to be for centuries has been inferior and incomplete to what its true purpose is. The church of Jesus Christ in the earth is God's training center for all believers where proven, mature and anointed leaders teach, mentor, develop and release God's people into the purpose of God for their lives. You are 'called' by Jesus Christ to become a mighty last day overcomer. The place where you are taught and trained to realize your potential is the church. When we have a teachable spirit combined with a submitted and faithful commitment to participate in a local church we will grow in grace and receive the reward of advancing in God's plan for our lives (being chosen).

It's important to have a proper attitude and understanding of the relationship between church members and church leaders. Recognize that church leaders have been called, chosen, anointed and set into their position by God. They are 'gifted' and anointed to bring great blessing and growth into your life. These men and women are not perfect, because they're human, just as you are. When you participate in a local church, it's important that you have an honoring, submitted and receptive heart toward the leaders. Remember that you're not doing this for men's sake, but because you're honoring and submitting to the anointed gift and grace God has placed in their life. Honor the position, anointing and gifting, because it is from God. We are all called to be submitted to spiritual leaders (including spiritual leaders themselves).

Hebrews 13:7, 17 (NKJV)

Remember those who rule over you, who have spoken the word of God to you, whose faith follow, considering the outcome of their conduct.

Obey those who rule over you, and be submissive, for they watch out for your souls, as those who must give account. Let them do so with joy and not with grief, for that would be unprofitable for you.

Hebrews 13:7, 17 (MSG)

Appreciate your pastoral leaders who gave you the Word of God. Take a good look at the way they live, and let their faithfulness instruct you, as well as their truthfulness.

Be responsive to your pastoral leaders. Listen to their counsel. They are alert to the condition of your lives and work under the strict supervision of God. Contribute to the joy of their leadership, not its drudgery. Why would you want to make things harder for them?

Hebrews 13:7, 17 (NLT)

Remember your leaders who taught you the word of God. Think of all the good that has come from their lives, and follow the example of their faith.

Obey your spiritual leaders, and do what they say. Their work is to watch over your souls, and they are accountable to God. Give them reason to do this with joy and not with sorrow. That would certainly not be for your benefit.

Leaders are called to lead by their example. They are called to be loving servants, not harsh dictators. The Lord is jealous over His beloved bride, the church, and brings into a strict discipline, those leaders who become abusive to His children. Vice-versa, when people become rebellious and divisive against the leadership of a church, it doesn't please God, because true spiritual leaders are a representation of God. He takes their mistreatment personally.

Psalm 105:15 (NKJV)

Saying, "Do not touch My anointed ones, and do My prophets no harm."

Psalm 105:15 (MSG)

"Don't you dare lay a hand on my anointed, don't hurt a hair on the heads of my prophets."

In case you're wondering, I also have a 'pastor' in my life, and have so for many years. I am genuinely submitted to the gift and grace that God has put in his life. My pastor has been a wonderful example to me of Christlikeness in his relationship with me. I have found that God looks approvingly at the heart that's submitted to His kingdom and the leaders He's ordained to cover and equip them. Both submission and rebellion are issues of the heart. The Lord doesn't want you to be afraid of making any decision in your life without asking your spiritual leaders. That's not the intent of God's heart for the life of the church. On the other hand, I've witnessed many people make life-altering decisions without even the thought of seeking the wisdom and prayer of their spiritual leaders. Many times their decisions have had devastating, personal consequences that might have been avoided if they had sought guidance from church leaders.

When we have a submissive heart, God sees it and brings His blessing into our lives.

I Peter 5:6 (NKJV)
Therefore humble yourselves under the mighty hand of God, that He may exalt you in due time . . .

I Peter 5:6 (AMP)
Therefore humble yourselves under the mighty hand of God, that He may exalt you in due time He may exalt you . . .

We humble ourselves under God's mighty hand by recognizing as absolute the Lordship of Christ and by making the Word of God the final authority over all our lives. The Word of God instructs us to be submitted to the ministry gifts Christ has set in the church (Apostles, Prophets, Evangelists, Pastors, Teachers) so the practical way that we humble ourselves under the mighty hand of God is through submitting to the five-fold ministry, like five fingers on God's hand.

God loves the church. Jesus birthed the church by His own blood. He is still building the church in the earth. Understand the importance and implacable purpose God has placed in the church. Resist the temptation to become critical or cynical about the church. If you've been hurt and have had a bad experience in church, recognize that human failure (in leaders and members) does not negate His plan for His people through the church. Don't give up on the church, God never will. His Word declares the promise of a 'glorious church.'

Ephesians 5:25-27 (NKJV)
Husbands, love your wives, just as Christ also loved the church and gave Himself for her, that He might sanctify and cleanse her with the washing of water by the word, that He might present her to Himself a glorious church, not having spot or wrinkle or any such thing, but that she should be holy and without blemish.

Jesus views the church as His bride. He loves the church and will do so for all eternity.

CHAPTER 9
QUESTIONS AND ANSWERS

1. Jesus Christ is the _____, _____ and _____ of the church.

2. The church belongs _____ _____ and He is the One that _____ _____.

3. The church in the earth today is comprised of every _____ _____ _____ in every _____, _____ and _____.

4. The five office gifts of this grace are _____, _____, _____, _____ and _____.

5. The purpose of these five office gifts is to _____, _____ and _____ people for their place of _____ in the body of Christ.

6. The church is to _____, _____ and _____ God's people in the ways and principles of _____ _____ and then to release them back to the world from which they were called out of as _____ _____ _____.

7. The Church of Jesus Christ on the earth is _____ _____ _____ for _____ _____.

8. When we have a _____ _____ combined with a _____ and _____ _____ to participate in a local church, we will _____ in _____ and receive the reward of advancing in _____ _____ for our lives.

9. Both _____ and _____ are issues of the _____.

10. We 'humble ourselves under God's mighty hand' by recognizing as absolute the _____ ____ _____ and by making the Word of God the _____ _____ over all our lives.

11. The practical way we humble ourselves under the mighty hand of God is through submitting to the _____ - _____ _____.

12. Jesus views the church as _____ _____.

10 THE KINGDOM

The message and ministry that Jesus Christ came to teach, preach and demonstrate is the gospel of the Kingdom of God. The first 'message' that He preached recorded in the New Testament is found in:

Matthew 4:17 (NKJV)
From that time Jesus began to preach and to say, "Repent, for the kingdom of heaven is at hand."

And also in Matthew 4:23 (NKJV)

And Jesus went about all Galilee, teaching in their synagogues, preaching the gospel of the kingdom, and healing all kinds of sickness and all kinds of disease among the people.

In over 100 parables and extended teachings Christ Jesus taught about the Kingdom of God in the four gospels. The truth of the Kingdom of God was the central focus of the ministry of Jesus Christ.

WHAT EXACTLY IS A KINGDOM?

A kingdom is the domain and dominion of a king. It is the territory, people and resource that He has unquestioned ownership and absolute authority over. In a kingdom, the word of the king is the sovereign law of the kingdom. Everything and everyone in the kingdom is under the king's complete control. The economic, social, medical and spiritual condition of the subjects of the kingdom are a direct reflection of the king. The king is represented and revealed by the quality of life he has provided for all those under his domain. In this sense, the kingdom itself and the king who reigns over it are one. If the king was generous, good and righteous, his kingdom and its subjects would benefit richly from the care he would show them. They, in turn, brought great satisfaction to the king by their prosperous lives and their gratitude for the kindness of their sovereign. But if a king (or queen) was cruel and evil, the subjects of the kingdom lived in the unending fearfulness of the horrors inflicted on them. Because of their complete dependence on the king for literally everything in their lives, every subject hoped and prayed for righteous and good monarchs. The people Christ preached to understood how kingdoms worked as they all lived under the Roman Empire.

WHAT IS THE KINGDOM OF GOD THAT JESUS PROCLAIMED?

The Kingdom of God is the reign and rulership of God in the hearts and lives of human beings through the Lordship of Jesus Christ in salvation and surrender. The Kingdom of God is the rule of God on earth. This wasn't a new idea or teaching, but was an extension and expansion of God's original covenant and mandate given to the first man and woman on earth. Man was created to bring the rulership (kingdom) of God to the earth.

Genesis 1:26-28 (NKJV) tells us

Then God said, "Let Us make man in Our image, according to Our likeness; let them have dominion over the fish of the sea, over the birds of the air, and over the cattle, over all the earth and over every creeping thing that creeps on the earth." So God created man in His own image; in the image of God He created him; male and female He created them. Then God blessed them, and God said to them, "Be fruitful and multiply; fill the earth and subdue it; have dominion over the fish of the sea, over the birds of the air, and over every living thing that moves on the earth."

God created the universe and its billions of galaxies and then turned His full attention to the centerpiece of His majestic creation, man (male and female) and the earth He created for man to live and rule in. He made us in 'His image and likeness'. We see His children carrying His image. Because man possessed the image of God, he was able to express the dominion (rule) of God to all of creation. This was God's design and also His delight, that His children would exercise His rule (kingdom) over the earth.

Psalm 115:16 (NKJV) tells us,

The heaven, even the heavens, are the LORD's; but the earth He has given to the children of men.

In the Garden of Eden, God literally gave mankind stewardship and authority over the earth. Man was to rule as a reflection of God, as His beloved children, as earthly ambassadors of the heavenly King and kingdom. This was God's original purpose for man and for a while it was beautifully accomplished until the most devastating day in all of history came, the day when man forfeited his purpose and partnership with God through sin. In our greatest imaginations we cannot comprehend and calculate how far we have fallen from who we were created to be and from what we were created to do. The universe itself is slowly dying because of man's sin. The world we live in is not the same world that God created. The resulting consequence of sin is powerfully evident in such things as sickness, suffering, injustice, violence, crime, pain, war and in countless other ways.

MAN'S BETRAYAL OF GOD IS HIGHLIGHTED IN SATAN'S TEMPTATION OF CHRIST.

Luke 4:5-7

Then the devil, taking Him up on a high mountain, showed Him all the kingdoms of the world in a moment of time. And the devil said to Him, "All this authority I will give You, and their glory; for this has been delivered to me, and I give it to whomever I wish. Therefore, if You will worship before me, all will be Yours."

And Jesus answered and said to him, "Get behind Me, Satan! For it is written, 'You shall worship the LORD your God, and Him only you shall serve.'"

Let us note first of all that if it couldn't have happened or legitimately been offered by Satan to Christ, it wouldn't have been a temptation, because it was untrue and unable to happen. So we then can summarize that Satan's offer to Christ was both true and legitimate, making it a real temptation.

In fact, the word Satan used for "delivered" is the Greek word paradidomi which means "to betray, surrender, entrust, transmit." Satan boldly declared to Christ that he was the legitimate ruler (king) over the kingdoms of the earth because the rightful authority over the earth had been 'betrayed" over to him by Adam. This represents the true picture of the oppression, chaos, and devastation mankind experienced as a result of the fall (original sin). Not only had man lost his rightful place of dominion on earth because of sin, in man's place the greatest enemy of God was now establishing his kingdom in place of God's. It was into this reality God sent His Son, Jesus Christ, over 2,000 years ago, to literally tear the keys of authority out of the hand of Satan and to reestablish God's original intent for man – that God's kingdom would reign in and through man.

Revelation 1:18 (NKJV)
I am He who lives, and was dead, and behold, I am alive forevermore. Amen. And I have the keys of Hades and of Death.

By the victory of Christ over sin and Satan, He restored the rulership of God in men and on earth. The curse is now broken by His great triumph!

Galatians 3:13-14 (NKJV)
Christ has redeemed us from the curse of the law, having become a curse for us (for it is written, "Cursed is everyone who hangs on a tree"), that the blessing of Abraham might come upon the Gentiles in Christ Jesus, that we might receive the promise of the Spirit through faith.

Colossians 1:13 (NKJV)

He has delivered us from the power of darkness and conveyed us into the kingdom of the Son of His love,

Salvation allows me to both see and then enter the glorious Kingdom of God.

John 3:3, 5 (NKJV)

Jesus answered and said to him, "Most assuredly, I say to you, unless one is born again, he cannot see the kingdom of God."

Jesus answered, "Most assuredly, I say to you, unless one is born of water and the Spirit, he cannot enter the kingdom of God.

WHERE IS THE KINGDOM OF GOD?

Jesus taught that God's kingdom wasn't in a location or building, but in the heart of man is where the rule of God is to be established.

Luke 17:20-21 (NKJV)

Now when He was asked by the Pharisees when the kingdom of God would come, He answered them and said, "The kingdom of God does not come with observation; nor will they say, 'See here!' or 'See there!' For indeed, the kingdom of God is within you."

After salvation (the regeneration of our spirit and the indwelling of the Holy Spirit through forgiveness of sin by the blood of Jesus), we have the opportunity and right to enter the Kingdom of God! We do so by responding in faith and obedience to the Word of the Kingdom.

Luke 16:16 (NKJV)

"The law and the prophets were until John. Since that time the kingdom of God has been preached, and everyone is pressing into it.

Pressing in is demonstrated by our unyielding faith, determined prayer and consistent confession concerning the promises of the Word of God. There is a required 'forcefulness' of heart and faith in the believer to fully experience the Kingdom.

Jesus said that the first priority of our lives and the prayers that flow from them must be to see the Kingdom of God come.

Matthew 6:9-10 (NKJV)
In this manner, therefore, pray: Our Father in heaven, hallowed be Your name. Your kingdom come. Your will be done on earth as it is in heaven.

Through the forcefulness of passionate prayer the Kingdom of God is expanded on earth.

Matthew 16:19 (NKJV)
And I will give you the keys of the kingdom of heaven, and whatever you bind on earth will be bound in heaven, and whatever you loose on earth will be loosed in heaven."

Matthew 16:19 (MSG)
"And that's not all. You will have complete and free access to God's kingdom, keys to open any and every door: no more barriers between heaven and earth, earth and heaven. A yes on earth is yes in heaven. A no on earth is no in heaven."

The 'Keys of the Kingdom' come through the revelation of God's Word in our heart. Every revelation produces a spiritual key that gives us authority to bind the works of Satan and sin and loose the will and Kingdom of God on earth. He entrusts us with keys with the expectation we will use them to accomplish His will by expanding His Kingdom.

The earthly administrator of the heavenly Kingdom of God is the person of the Holy Spirit. Jesus promised and then sent the beautiful dove of heaven to us.

Romans 14:17 (NKJV)
...for the kingdom of God is not eating and drinking, but righteousness and peace and joy in the Holy Spirit.

The Holy Spirit gives believers righteousness, peace and joy which are graces of the

Kingdom of God.

THE MISSING PIECE: THE 7 MOUNTAIN STRATEGY

One of the most important understandings of the nature, purpose and power of the Kingdom of God is found in the teaching of "The 7 Mountains." This powerful revelation begins with the prophecies of scripture in

Isaiah 2:2-3 (NKJV)

Now it shall come to pass in the latter days that the mountain of the LORD's house shall be established on the top of the mountains, and shall be exalted above the hills; and all nations shall flow to it.

Many people shall come and say, "Come, and let us go up to the mountain of the LORD, to the house of the God of Jacob; He will teach us His ways, and we shall walk in His paths." For out of Zion shall go forth the law, and the word of the LORD from Jerusalem.

In Scripture, mountains are a metaphor for kingdoms. This scripture tells us that God's Kingdom would be exalted above all other kingdoms (mountains and hills). This is much more than a millennial promise for when Christ comes back again in the consummation of the Kingdom. It is a prophecy for now. The Kingdom of God will be exalted above all other kingdoms through believers like you and me who will bring His Kingdom into these other kingdoms.

Daniel 2:44 (NKJV)

And in the days of these kings the God of heaven will set up a kingdom which shall never be destroyed; and the kingdom shall not be left to other people; it shall break in pieces and consume all these kingdoms, and it shall stand forever.

This is God's great end-time plan, that His people will rise up and experience and enforce the great victory of the cross by revealing and releasing the power of God's Kingdom to mankind.

Psalm 110:1-3 (NKJV)

The LORD said to my Lord, "Sit at My right hand, till I make Your enemies Your footstool."

The LORD shall send the rod of Your strength out of Zion. Rule in the midst of Your enemies!

Your people shall be volunteers in the day of Your power; in the beauties of holiness, from the womb of the morning, You have the dew of Your youth.

The children of Israel were miraculously delivered from Egypt by the mighty arm of God. The Passover was the final great instrument of deliverance when the Israelites put the blood of a blemishless lamb on the doorposts of their homes. That evening, the judgment of God fell on every house in Egypt that was not covered with the blood of a lamb. This is a beautiful portrait of our glorious salvation through the precious blood of the Lamb of God, Jesus Christ, who died for the sins of mankind. As they exited Egypt, Pharoah and the Egyptian army came after them one more time, only to be drowned in the Red Sea. This is a picture of what happens in water baptism when the power of the enemy and the bondage of our past are removed.

As the Hebrews began their journey, God opened water from the rock when they were thirsty, and fed them heavenly manna every morning for food (a picture of God's Word feeding our souls). During the day a mighty cloud gave them protection from the desert heat, and at night an awesome pillar of fire protected them from cold and predators. Every need was met as they experienced the sublime grace of their loving God.

But here's the problem they had, and many times what the church has had throughout history. God brought them out of Egypt so He could bring them into the promised land. The wilderness was to only be the place of transition, preparation and transformation between Egypt (a type of the world) and Canaan (a picture of living in the Kingdom of God). When the Lord gave them the instructions to enter into Canaan, drive out the inhabitants, and to take possession in their place, the children of Israel said, "no thanks." They didn't 'get it' then and many don't 'get it' now. We've been saved for a kingdom purpose and assignment. Notice the dynamic in the children of Israel in Numbers 13:27-33 (NKJV):

Then they told him, and said: "We went to the land where you sent us. It truly flows with milk and honey, and this is its fruit. Nevertheless the people who dwell in the land are strong; the cities are fortified and very large; moreover we saw the descendants of Anak there. The Amalekites dwell in the land of the South; the Hittites, the Jebusites, and the Amorites dwell in the mountains; and the Canaanites dwell by the sea and along the banks of the Jordan."

Then Caleb quieted the people before Moses, and said, "Let us go up at once and take possession, for we are well able to overcome it."

But the men who had gone up with him said, "We are not able to go up against the people, for they are stronger than we." And they gave the children of Israel a bad report of the land which they had spied out, saying, "The land through which we have gone as spies is a land that devours its inhabitants, and all the people whom we saw in it are men of great stature. There we saw the giants (the descendants of Anak came from the giants); and we were like grasshoppers in our own sight, and so we were in their sight."

Hebrews 3:7-11, 19

Therefore, as the Holy Spirit says: "Today, if you will hear His voice,

Do not harden your hearts as in the rebellion, in the day of trial in the wilderness, where your fathers tested Me, tried Me, and saw My works forty years.

Therefore I was angry with that generation, and said, 'They always go astray in their heart, and they have not known My ways.'

So I swore in My wrath, 'They shall not enter My rest.'"

So we see that they could not enter in because of unbelief.

Although they were in open rebellion and disobedience against God's will, He refused to change His mind, but simply waited for another generation to arise and fulfill His purpose. Forty years later another generation was given the same 'word' from God to cross the river Jordan and take possession of the promised land.

Joshua 1:1-3 (NKJV)

After the death of Moses the servant of the LORD, it came to pass that the LORD spoke to Joshua the son of Nun, Moses' assistant, saying: "Moses My servant is dead. Now therefore, arise, go over this Jordan, you and all this people, to the land which I am giving to them—the children of Israel. Every place that the sole of your foot will tread upon I have given you, as I said to Moses.

This is who we are, the 'Joshua Generation,' called to conquer Canaan and bring God's rule to the kingdoms of the earth. In Canaan there were seven nations that Israel had to dispossess in order to take the land. These seven nations represent the seven mountains of human activity and authority. All of people's lives are represented in these seven mountains. These are the mountains that we are called to 'conquer' for the Kingdom of God.

Deut. 7:1-6 (NKJV)
"When the LORD your God brings you into the land which you go to possess, and has cast out many nations before you, the Hittites and the Girgashites and the Amorites and the Canaanites and the Perizzites and the Hivites and the Jebusites, seven nations greater and mightier than you, and when the LORD your God delivers them over to you, you shall conquer them and utterly destroy them. You shall make no covenant with them nor show mercy to them. Nor shall you make marriages with them. You shall not give your daughter to their son, nor take their daughter for your son. For they will turn your sons away from following Me, to serve other gods; so the anger of the LORD will be aroused against you and destroy you suddenly. But thus you shall deal with them: you shall destroy their altars, and break down their sacred pillars, and cut down their wooden images, and burn their carved images with fire.

"For you are a holy people to the LORD your God; the LORD your God has chosen you to be a people for Himself, a special treasure above all the peoples on the face of the earth.

Deut. 20:16-18 (NKJV)
"But of the cities of these peoples which the LORD your God gives you as an inheritance, you shall let nothing that breathes remain alive, but you shall utterly destroy them: the Hittite and the Amorite and the Canaanite and the Perizzite and the Hivite and the Jebusite, just as the LORD your God has commanded you, lest they teach you to do according to all their abominations which they have done for their gods, and you sin against the LORD your God.

THE 7 MOUNTAINS

Mountains	Strongholds	Tribe
1. Family	Discouragement	Jebusites
2. Church	Pride	Amorites
3. Business	Greed	Canaanites
4. Education	Humanism	Hivites
5. Government	Corruption	Girgashites
6. Media	Fear	Hittites
7. Arts/Entertainment	Immorality	Perizzites

Every 'mountain' has a unique stronghold that must be addressed and overcome in order for the Kingdom of God to possess it. This means that we must both individually and then corporately defeat the strongholds in our own lives, families and churches to have authority to establish God's Kingdom in that mountain.

What mountain are you called to conquer for the kingdom? Caleb knew his mountain and refused to die before he had taken it.

Joshua 14:6-15 (NKJV)

Then the children of Judah came to Joshua in Gilgal. And Caleb the son of Jephunneh the Kenizzite said to him: "You know the word which the LORD said to Moses the man of God concerning you and me in Kadesh Barnea. I was forty years old when Moses the servant of the LORD sent me from Kadesh Barnea to spy out the land, and I brought back word to him as it was in my heart. Nevertheless my brethren who went up with me made the heart of the people melt, but I wholly followed the LORD my God. So Moses swore on that day, saying, 'Surely the land where your foot has trodden shall be your inheritance and your children's forever, because you have wholly followed the LORD my God.' And now, behold, the LORD has kept me alive, as He said, these forty-five years, ever since the LORD spoke this word to Moses while Israel wandered in the wilderness; and now, here I am this day, eighty-five years old. As yet I am as strong this day as on the day that Moses sent me; just as my strength was then, so now is my strength for war, both for going out and for coming in. Now therefore, give me this mountain of which the LORD spoke in that day; for you heard in that day how the Anakim were there, and that the cities were great and fortified. It may be that the LORD will be with me, and I shall be able to drive them out as the LORD said."

And Joshua blessed him, and gave Hebron to Caleb the son of Jephunneh as an inheritance. Hebron therefore became the inheritance of Caleb the son of Jephunneh the Kenizzite to this day, because he wholly followed the LORD God of Israel. And the name of Hebron formerly was Kirjath Arba (Arba was the greatest man among the Anakim).

Then the land had rest from war.

Caleb's great request, "Now therefore, GIVE ME THIS MOUNTAIN," must also be the cry of our heart to God. You've been called to bring the Kingdom of God to at least one of these mountain kingdoms, possibly several of them.

Seek the Lord for which 'kingdom' is your destiny to conquer for the Kingdom. This is the purpose God has ordained for His beloved church, to bring the rule of His Kingdom into every kingdom of men.

Matthew 11:12 (NKJV)
And from the days of John the Baptist until now the kingdom of heaven suffers violence, and the violent take it by force.

CHAPTER 10
QUESTIONS & ANSWERS

1. The message and ministry that Jesus Christ came to teach, preach and demonstrate is the _____ ___ ___ _____ ____ _____.

2. A kingdom is the _____ and _____ of a king.

3. In a kingdom, the _____ ___ ___ _____ is the sovereign law of the kingdom.

4. The Kingdom of God is the _____ and _____ of God in the _____ and _____ of human beings through the _____ ___ _____ _____ in salvation and surrender.

5. Psalm 115:16 tells us, "The heaven, even the heavens are the LORD'S; But the _____ He has given to the _____ ___ _____."

6. Satan boldly declared to Christ that he was the legitimate ruler (king) over the _____ __ ___ _____ because the rightful authority over the earth had been "_____" over to him by Adam.

7. By the victory of Christ over _____ and _____ He restored the _____ ___ _____ in men _____ on earth.

8. The "keys of the kingdom" come through the _____ ___ _____ _____ in our heart. Every _____ produces a _____ _____ that gives us _____ to bind the works of Satan and sin and loose the will and _____ ___ _____ on earth.

9. In Scripture, mountains are a metaphor for _____.

10. This is God's great end-time plan, that His people will rise up and _____ and _____ of the cross by _____ and _____ the power of _____ _____ to mankind.

11. God brought them (Israel) out of Egypt so He could bring them into the _____ _____.

12. In Canaan there were 7 nations that Israel had to _____ in order to take the ___ _____ ___ _____ _____ and _____.

13. List the 7 mountains and their strongholds.

Mountains   Strongholds

1.

2.

3.

4.

5.

6.

7.

14. Caleb's great request, "Now therefore, _____ _____ ____ _____"
must also be the cry of our heart to God.

15. You've been called to bring the _____ ___ _____ to at least one of
these mountain kingdoms, possibly several of them.

16. Seek the Lord for which "_____" is your _____ ___ _____
for the kingdom.

17. Matthew 11:12
And from the days of John the Baptist until now the kingdom of heaven suffers violence,
and the violent _____ ___ ___ _____.

DR. MICHAEL MAIDEN

Dr. Michael Maiden and Mary, his beloved wife of over 35 years, are the senior pastors of Church for the Nations in Phoenix, Arizona. Here he strongly and lovingly prepares God's people for service in God's Kingdom. The messages are always relevant, timely and life-changing as well as prophetic.

Dr. Maiden has earned both a Masters and Doctorate Degree in Christian Psychology. He has authored seven books including: The Joshua Generation: God's Manifesto for the End Time Church, and his most recent book, Turn the World Upside Down, which speaks to this present generation about the next step to be taken.

In addition to his work in the local church, he is a strong prophetic voice to this generation and has ministered to those holding Public Offices as well as Pastors and Ministers throughout the world. Dr. Maiden is President and CEO of Church On The Rock International – a dynamic ministry that oversees more than 6,000 churches worldwide. He is also on the board of Fishers of Men International, the Jewish Voice International and several local churches.